the series on school ref

Patricia A. Wasley	Ann Lieberman	Josep..
University of Washington	Carnegie Foundation for the Advancement of Teaching	New York University

SERIES EDITORS

The Mindful Teacher
ELIZABETH MACDONALD & DENNIS SHIRLEY

Going to Scale with New School Designs:
Reinventing High School
JOSEPH P. MCDONALD, EMILY J. KLEIN, &
MEG RIORDAN

Managing to Change: How Schools Can Survive
(and Sometimes Thrive) in Turbulent Times
THOMAS HATCH

Teacher Practice Online:
Sharing Wisdom, Opening Doors
DÉSIRÉE H. POINTER MACE

Teaching the Way Children Learn
BEVERLY FALK

Teachers in Professional Communities:
Improving Teaching and Learning
ANN LIEBERMAN & LYNNE MILLER, EDS.

Looking Together at Student Work, 2nd Ed.
TINA BLYTHE, DAVID ALLEN, &
BARBARA SCHIEFFELIN POWELL

The Power of Protocols: An Educator's Guide to
Better Practice, 2nd Ed.
JOSEPH P. MCDONALD, NANCY MOHR,
ALAN DICHTER, & ELIZABETH C. MCDONALD

Schools-within-Schools: Possibilities and Pitfalls of
High School Reform
VALERIE E. LEE & DOUGLAS D. READY

Seeing Through Teachers' Eyes: Professional Ideals
and Classroom Practices
KAREN HAMMERNESS

Building School-Based Teacher Learning
Communities: Professional Strategies to Improve
Student Achievement
MILBREY MCLAUGHLIN & JOAN TALBERT

Mentors in the Making: Developing New Leaders
for New Teachers
BETTY ACHINSTEIN &
STEVEN Z. ATHANASES, EDS.

Community in the Making: Lincoln Center
Institute, the Arts, and Teacher Education
MADELEINE FUCHS HOLZER &
SCOTT NOPPE-BRANDON, EDS.

Holding Accountability Accountable:
What Ought to Matter in Public Education
KENNETH A. SIROTNIK, ED.

Mobilizing Citizens for Better Schools
ROBERT F. SEXTON

The Comprehensive High School Today
FLOYD M. HAMMACK, ED.

The Teaching Career
JOHN I. GOODLAD &
TIMOTHY J. MCMANNON, EDS.

Beating the Odds: High Schools as Communities
of Commitment
JACQUELINE ANCESS

At the Heart of Teaching: A Guide to
Reflective Practice
GRACE HALL MCENTEE, JON APPLEBY,
JOANNE DOWD, JAN GRANT, SIMON HOLE, &
PEGGY SILVA, WITH JOSEPH W. CHECK

Teaching Youth Media: A Critical Guide to Literacy,
Video Production, and Social Change
STEVEN GOODMAN

Inside the National Writing Project: Connecting
Network Learning and Classroom Teaching
ANN LIEBERMAN & DIANE WOOD

Standards Reform in High-Poverty Schools:
Managing Conflict and Building Capacity
CAROL A. BARNES

Standards of Mind and Heart:
Creating the Good High School
PEGGY SILVA & ROBERT A. MACKIN

Upstart Startup:
Creating and Sustaining a Public Charter School
JAMES NEHRING

One Kid at a Time: Big Lessons from a Small School
ELIOT LEVINE

Guiding School Change:
The Role and Work of Change Agents
FRANCES O'CONNELL RUST &
HELEN FREIDUS, EDS.

Teachers Caught in the Action: Professional
Development That Matters
ANN LIEBERMAN & LYNNE MILLER, EDS.

(Continued)

the series on school reform, *continued*

THE

MINDFUL

TEACHER

Elizabeth MacDonald
Dennis Shirley

TEACHERS
COLLEGE
PRESS

Teachers College, Columbia University
New York and London

Published by Teachers College Press, 1234 Amsterdam Avenue, New York, NY 10027

Library of Congress Cataloging-in-Publication Data

MacDonald, Elizabeth.
 The mindful teacher / Elizabeth MacDonald, Dennis Shirley.
   p. cm.
 Includes bibliographical references and index.
 ISBN 978-0-8077-5019-3 (pbk. : alk. paper)
 1. Reflective teaching. 2. Buddhism and education. 3. Teaching—Psychological aspects.
I. Shirley, Dennis, 1955- II. Title.
 LB1027.22.M34 2010
 371.102—dc22

                                                          2009020601

ISBN 978-0-8077-5019-3 (paperback)

Printed on acid-free paper
Manufactured in the United States of America

16 15 14 13 12 11 10 09   8 7 6 5 4 3 2 1

Dedicated with great affection to all of our students.

Contents

Acknowledgments

OUR FIRST THANKS go to the funders and selection committee members of the Boston Collaborative Fellows Grant. This innovative grant encourages professors in the Lynch School of Education at Boston College to conduct collaborative research with their colleagues in the Boston Public Schools. The selection committee is made up of an equal number of Lynch School and Boston Public School faculty and administrators. Without the generous support of this grant the Mindful Teacher project would not have been possible.

We have also benefited from several other foundations and centers that have supported one or both of us for research and reflection. These include the Rockefeller Foundation's Study and Conference Center in Bellagio, Italy; the Alexander von Humboldt Foundation in Bonn, Germany; the Freudenberg Foundation in Weinheim, Germany; the Bosch Foundation in Stuttgart, Germany; and the Scholars' Forum of the Public Education Network in Washington, DC. Special thanks go to the Lilly Foundation in Indianapolis, which provided funding for a program at Boston College entitled "Intersections" that in many ways served as the catalyst for the Mindful Teacher seminars.

We would like to express our gratitude to the many friends and colleagues who participated in the Mindful Teacher seminars and who contributed to this volume. They include Caitlyn Albano, Leylah Antunez, Karyn Cirulli, Rita Dip-Rossi, Julie Flaherty, Rebecca Fischer, Jill Freiberg, Yeshi Gaskin, Adam Koneman, Megan Mahoney, Dean Martin, LaTanya Moore, Eric Meuse, Victoria Megias-Batista, Janet Nicholson-Cronin, Heather Page, Adriana Rodriguez, Renee Simmons, Maggie Slye, Dale Sudeall, Jeff Timberlake, Patricia Travers, and Edward Urban. We thank the teachers in the Boston Public Schools and especially those at James A. Garfield School. Critical friends Jean Anyon, Maria Estela Brisk, Rosellen Brown, Patricia Cooper, Dean Fink, Afra Hersi, Marvin Hoffman, Janice Jackson, Ellen Langer, Ann Lieberman, Edvin Østergaard, Thomas Payzant, Fran Peterman, Michael Schratz, Alison Skerrett, and Wiel Veugelers each were helpful in providing valuable comments either by meeting with us in person or by carefully reading early drafts of the final manuscript. Other friends and colleagues, too numerous to name, read earlier versions of this manuscript and advised us with their criticisms and commentaries that greatly improved the final version. We are especially grateful to Marie Ellen Larcada of Teachers College Press for establishing contact with us at an annual meeting of the American Educational Research Association, expressing immediate interest in our work, and guiding us in our writing of this book both expertly and all the way to its conclusion.

We would like to thank the following Boston College students for the enthusiasm and expertise they brought to this project: Michele Clancy, Mike DiLuzio, Molly Dugan, Marlene Gomez, Gloria Knight, Randall Lahann, and Kathryn Sallis. One of us completed a separate volume with Andy Hargreaves entitled *The Fourth Way: The Inspiring Future of Educational Change* 6 weeks before this manuscript was finished, and this volume benefited greatly from his friendship and wisdom.

To affect the quality of the day, that is the highest of arts.

—Henry David Thoreau, *Walden*

Introduction

THE CONCEPT OF "mindfulness" currently is experiencing enormous popular resonance in American society. Ellen Langer, a Harvard psychologist, has made mindfulness the topic of two best-selling books, *Mindfulness* (1989) and *The Power of Mindful Learning* (1997). Thich Nhat Hanh, a Vietnamese Buddhist monk who was nominated by Martin Luther King for the Nobel Peace Prize in 1967, has become a best-selling author, with books translated into many languages, advocating the healing power of mindful meditation and affiliated "mindfulness trainings" designed to bring peace and serenity to everyday life (Hanh, 2001). Whether one is a Harvard savant or an Eastern sage, it would appear that there is great popular desire for more mindfulness in our society at this historical moment.

And why not? Scholars in the field of "subjective well-being" can produce mountains of data documenting that our fast-paced, stretched-thin lifestyles are correlated with a soaring rise in depression and a loss of locus of control (Lane, 2000; Seligman, 2002). Although the greatest determinant of our happiness in many ways has to do with the quality of our interpersonal relationships, a booming advertising industry perpetually tries to persuade us that our greatest pleasures are to be found in consumption—and we all too often act as if we believe this were true, sacrificing our relationships with friends and family in pursuit of material gratification. The contemporary credit crisis and recession are only the economic manifestation of a larger societal crisis of values that has now reached virtually every corner of the globe. Small wonder that "mindfulness" is attractive to people who are looking for some deeper meaning in their lives yet who are reluctant to give themselves over to fundamentalist religious movements, cults, or other forms of group membership that appear to mitigate against critical thinking and individualism.

Paradoxically, in spite of this great appeal on numerous levels, with all kinds of seminars and retreats sponsoring a cottage industry promoting a variety of contemplative practices, mindfulness appears to be a relatively underdeveloped, if not altogether peripheral, concept in terms of main-

1

stream educational practice and research. Rather, a host of new standards-driven "reforms" have conspired to make thoughtful teaching in our public schools—entailing rich curricula adapted to the needs and personalities of particular students—harder and harder for teachers to practice. The new policy imperative to practice "data-driven decision making" (DDDM) has led many educators to believe that they are "drowning" in the wrong kinds of data—the kinds that not only shame struggling schools, but are processed and returned to schools by testing agencies too late to have any instructional value for the individual pupils who were tested (Celio & Harvey, 2005; Ingram, Seashore Louis, & Schroeder, 2004). As a consequence of the "standards stampede" (Hargreaves, 2003, p. 176) of the past 20 years, now teachers often find themselves forced to keep up with district- and state-mandated "pacing guides" even when their students have not fully understood the material in the timeline indicated by the guides. Educational leaders, under the gun to achieve "adequate yearly progress" to meet No Child Left Behind (NCLB) indicators, respond by telling teachers to focus on "bubble kids" who will bump a school's scores up above a given cut score—abandoning the traditional moral imperative of educators to teach all pupils (Booher-Jennings, 2005; Pedulla et al., 2003). At the higher education level, policymakers seek to place pressure on colleges and universities to prove that they are "adding value" in terms of raising students' academic achievement (Spellings Commission, 2006). As accountability becomes transformed into accountancy, science turns into scientism, and the legitimate drive for academic achievement becomes narrowed into a single-minded obsession with test scores, what possibilities remain for ethical, caring teachers to hone their craft and to inspire their students with the sheer joy and delight that is to be found in learning?

ALIENATED TEACHING

This volume is intended to explore this question, using the following approach. First, we will describe what we conceptualize as "alienated teaching." From our perspective, alienated teaching now is endemic in American schools. In a nutshell, alienated teaching is a kind of teaching that teachers perform when they feel that they *must* comply with external conditions that they have not chosen and from which they inwardly dissent because they feel that new reforms do not serve their children well. Alienated teaching has many different modalities, which we will map out in the pages that follow. In part, we will argue, alienated teaching is a consequence of ever-intensifying new policy mandates at the district, state, and federal levels; in part, it is a result of educators' sense that their teaching practices are not really addressing critical, long-standing inequities in American schools and society; in part, it is a result of educators' own (often unconscious) capitulation to egregious tendencies in American society that undermine their own moral purpose and sense of efficacy.

How should teachers respond to district policies that prescribe a certain number of hours of instruction in each content area, when those hours exceed the actual number of hours they have in class with their pupils each week? How should teachers act when curricular packages are prescribed that they feel certain will engage their students but also valorize forms of learning that will not be measured on standardized tests? How should teachers cope with the rhetoric of data-driven decision making that appears to negate the many prosaic but nonetheless profoundly influential interactions that pupils have with their peers on a daily basis that can enhance or undermine learning? How can teachers even begin to focus on instruction when their pupils bring emotional issues from unstable home situations into the classroom that cry out for a gentle, reassuring touch from the one adult that they seem to have some stable and regular contact with on a daily basis?

These kinds of questions rarely are addressed in teacher professional development workshops today, which have become more and more focused on unidimensional forms of assessment and in many ways have parsed students' complicated lives outside of schools altogether out of sustained inquiry by teachers. In addition, a great deal of research on school improvement focuses on issues of alignment between pedagogy, curricula, and assessment, without acknowledging that in a tumultuous policy environment, few (if any) schools enjoy such alignment. In one recent study by the RAND Corporation, a majority of elementary school teachers felt that math and science standards in their states "include more content than can be covered adequately in the school year" (Hamilton et al., 2007, p. 43). "In such a situation," the researchers noted, "teachers must decide on their own whether to cover some standards fully and omit others or whether to cover all the standards incompletely" (p. 43). In addition, significant minorities (on the order of 20–30%) of elementary teachers believed that the standards "do not cover some important content areas." The authors continued, "These teachers faced the dilemma of teaching the content though it was not included in the standards and would not be on the assessment or omitting the content though they believed it was important" (p. 43). Individual classroom teachers cannot change the overall policy environment, and given the dilemmas that they face, no amount of data can "drive" them to resolve these complicated decisions in ways that involve a complex variety of trade-offs, all of which have important ethical

ramifications. But much of the dominant rhetoric of pupil achievement today suggests that they should indeed be so driven, thereby extending and
exacerbating the phenomenon of alienated teaching.

MINDFUL TEACHING

To overcome alienated teaching, we will propose in this book an alternative conception of "mindful teaching," in which teachers struggle to attain
congruence, integrity, and efficacy in their practice. Mindful teaching, in
this account, is not a program that can be purchased, a recipe that can be
followed, or a "silver bullet" that can be fired into your instruction to raise
your test scores. Rather, it is a form of teaching that is informed by contemplative practices and teacher inquiry that enables teachers to interrupt
their harried lifestyles, come to themselves through participation in a collegial community of inquiry and practice, and attend to aspects of their
classroom instruction and pupils' learning that ordinarily are overlooked
in the press of events.

As is the case with alienated teaching, mindful teaching can take a
variety of forms. We explore these here not through prescription but
through description and analysis. The heart of the discussion takes place
in an investigation of six "anchoring illustrations" of mindful teaching in
Chapter 3 and "seven synergies" and "triple tensions" of mindful teaching
in Chapter 4.

THE MINDFUL TEACHER SEMINARS

From whence do we derive our data for our descriptions of alienated and
mindful teaching? For the past 4 years we have led a series of seminars
entitled "The Mindful Teacher" that has enabled us to gather together two
cohorts of urban public school teachers in Boston to inquire into their
craft. Abandoning orthodox professional development structures and ap-
propriating participatory research strategies that would provide multiple
opportunities for teachers themselves to generate new findings (Cochran-
Smith & Lytle, 1993, 2009), we determined at the outset that we would
not articulate pre-established outcomes for the seminar. Rather, our goal
would be to establish maximum openness for teachers to identify and to
explore collaboratively what *they* experience as core dilemmas and problems in their practice; to address the whole host of issues that emerge
in the urban environment that make it difficult for their pupils to excel;
and to keep a fluid structure so that new topics could emerge continually

and be taken up by our cohorts in ways that would advance their aware-ness and deepen their understanding of the complexities of teaching and learning. Aware of the many barriers that have separated university from school-based faculty, we would write a book in which a classroom teacher and a higher education faculty member would take the lead, but in which the two cohorts of teachers played a major role in providing ideas and commentaries through a structure of "sustained interactivity" (Huber-man, 1999) over time, so that the final product in many ways would be the manifestation of a collaborative venture.

THE GREAT DIVIDE

Why did we plan and lead our Mindful Teacher seminars? In large part, these seminars were initiated by a comment once made by a veteran ur-ban educator who told a group of higher education faculty something like the following: "You at the university level have really good questions and do really good research, but *your* questions aren't *our* questions." If this remark is true—and countless conversations with teachers would seem to indicate that it does have a ring of truth to it—what *are* teachers' ques-tions? Why is there such a "great divide" between teachers and research-ers? Why is it so hard for teachers' questions to be asked in common activity settings, for example, in teachers' lounges, where teachers could pool their craft wisdom, come up with potential solutions, and then try out new strategies and evaluate them?

We suggest that it has to do with the strange culture of educational change that has been created, not only in the United States, but in vir-tually all advanced industrialized nations. When one first enters teach-ing, one is excited by new opportunities that emerge. One learns of new district initiatives, often with outside philanthropic support, and eagerly pursues the earliest trainings to get ahead of the curve and to push for-ward with innovative practices. This can be a time of experimentation, adaptation, and genuine intellectual excitement (Evans, 2001).

Over time, however, as one becomes more experienced, one begins to note disturbing patterns. New superintendents arrive, with new curricu-lar packages to implement and little knowledge of previous undertakings; policy makers push reforms, often in the form of short 1- or 2-year grants, that seem to come and go with meager research support and little under-standing of the on-the-ground realities of real classrooms in real schools; teachers' own ideas and experiences often are overlooked, with greater acknowledgment awarded to more prestigious (and well-funded) outsid-ers; in some cases, older curricula actually are locked up in closets or removed from buildings altogether so that teachers are forced to use new and often untested curricula. Few policy makers seem to understand that teachers are attracted to the profession primarily by its psychic rewards, and that top-down reforms need to be balanced with bottom-up creativity and initiative. Looking over the past 2 decades of school "reform," we see teachers who have been total-quality managed, shared-decision-making trained, outcomes-based-education restructured, computer-enhanced instructioned, and whole-school-improvement planned. Teachers have been reader and writer workshopped, constructivist math investigated, and school and university partnered. Is it any wonder that so many experienced teachers have become weary of what change management scholar Eric Abrahamson (2004) has described as "repetitive change syndrome," and have decided to withdraw behind the closed doors of their classrooms, where they hone their craft in private?

THE UNHOLY TRINITY

At a very personal level, the launching of the Mindful Teacher seminars was an effort for both of us to battle the kind of cynicism and resignation that bedevils far too many experienced educators—and that (in point of fact) we found ourselves falling prey to. Decades ago, sociologist Dan Lortie (1975) described teachers as caught up in an unholy trinity of conservatism, individualism, and presentism. In the uncertain environment of the classroom, teachers became conservative insofar as they clutched onto what worked, and developed an intrinsic distaste for new reforms; they became individualistic because of the cellular nature of teaching and lack of opportunities to observe colleagues and swap ideas; and they fell prey to presentism because administrators failed to include them in long-term plans, so they simply focused on the day-to-day without being able to participate in the shaping of a broader common culture that could evolve over time.

Since Lortie's publication of *Schoolteacher: A Sociological Study*, teachers, researchers, and policy makers have endeavored to shake up the unholy trinity and to help teachers to become more open to change, more collegial, and more active in the shaping of school cultures in not just the short term, but also the medium and long term. In many ways, these efforts have been successful, as teacher inquiry groups—alternately called "professional learning communities," "communities of learners," or "teacher leadership teams"—have proliferated (Lieberman & Miller, 2008; Stoll et al., 2006). In the very best cases, these kinds of new horizontal structures and cultures in schools have provided teachers with badly needed emotional support, enabled them to gain new ideas to incorporate into their classrooms, promoted a sense among teachers of being responsible for all of the children in the building (not just those in their classes), and given them access to scholarship so that they can thoughtfully integrate new research findings into their long-standing repertoires of classroom activities (Bryk & Schneider, 2004; Lieberman & Wood, 2003; McLaughlin & Talbert, 2001; Newmann & Wehlage, 1995). A growing body of research indicates that when teachers have such activity settings—when they really are able to support one another with challenging instructional issues and can collaborate to expand their learning about possible responses—pupil learning does indeed benefit (Chen, Heritage, & Lee, 2005; Hargreaves et al., 2007; Symonds, 2003).

In other cases, however, even the best of reforms became tainted by problems of implementation and building-level barriers to change (McQuillan, 1998; Payne, 2008). Rather than providing teachers with the opportunity and resources for meaningful collaboration, in some cases educational leaders mandated structural reforms without any accompanying attention to culture, inadvertently creating a kind of "contrived collegiality" that only reinforced teacher cynicism (Hargreaves, 1994, p. 186). Because the rise of professional learning communities occurred concurrently with the rise of the accountability movement, the openness that appeared to be promised through genuine teacher collaboration easily became captive to the drive to study and then increase pupil test scores (Hargreaves & Shirley, 2009b). The concerns of teachers who had other issues— for example, what to do with a child whose mother was a crack addict and who attended school irregularly, how to defuse a conflict between two boys that seemed to escalate into a fight every Friday after lunch with clockwork regularity, or how to encourage children to develop their own curricular themes and interests—were viewed as distractions to the tough-sounding, "laser-like" focus on instruction.

Furthermore, many policy makers and upper-level administrators seemed to miss irony entailed in many of the reforms promoting teacher inquiry. If these reforms were to entail a genuine empowerment of teachers and a shift to a more transformational paradigm with distributed leadership, then upper-level administrators would need to modify their more traditional and transactional approaches (Friedman, 2004). Yet high-stakes testing environments hardly encouraged principals to take short-term risks that might yield long-term gains (Hargreaves & Shirley, 2009b). When they failed to do so, teachers responded with a sense of betrayal, once again exacerbating the mutually reinforcing microcultures of conservativism, individualism, and presentism.

Thus far in this account it might seem that teachers are the innocent victims of Machiavellian policy makers, Draconian administrators, and Voldemortian test designers. In point of fact, we do indeed believe that far too many pressures have been placed upon classroom teachers, and that the unrealistically high burdens are a major source of the extraordinarily high rate of teacher attrition in our schools. Yet simply blaming others is far too easy. In a constitutional republic like our own, educators are very much public servants; we are the ultimate "street-level democrats" (Shirley, 2006b). Teachers themselves, through the advocacy of the American Federation of Teachers, played a major role in promoting and advancing standards-based reforms over the past 2 decades (Ravitch, 2000). Educators need to understand the sometimes desperate sense of public urgency about school improvement, especially given the "silent epidemic" of high school dropouts that generates millions of unskilled workers for a new "knowledge economy" that is mercilessly harsh on the poorly educated (Bridgeland, DiIulio, & Morison, 2006). Knee-jerk rebellion, in the form of those teachers who cross their arms and say "make me!" when learning about new practices that really could benefit their pupils, can be just as mindless and limiting as unreflective compliance.

The point, rather, is that teachers, as professionals, need a cultural space and time (always at a premium!) in which they can share instructional problems, select and modify curricula, and review, discuss, and use data to improve pupil achievement. Teachers need activity settings in which they can think together and develop increasingly sophisticated levels of awareness about the full range of instructional options that they possess, especially when trying to engage students in learning who (for whatever reasons) have given up on themselves or have developed anti-school ideologies of their own. Teachers possess disparate philosophies of education, and without opportunities for debating and clarifying the strengths and potential limitations of each perspective, their deeply held differences can lead to corrosive adversarial relationships that undermine community and relational trust (Achinstein, 2002). With such activity settings, on the other hand, teachers can attack the root problems causing alienated teaching and pupil resistance to schools, and by continually reflecting upon and modifying their work, can improve it, not only reaching their pupils more effectively, but also drawing more satisfaction and indeed fulfillment from their vocations (Palmer, 1998).

In point of fact, this book provides one such activity setting; it is the product of many years of collaboration between a classroom teacher and a university professor. In composing the book, we have worked hard to combine a sense of the on-the-ground reality and expertise of an urban teacher with the analytical and writing skills of a higher education colleague. While the entire book is the manifestation of this collaboration, at times the teacher's voice will dominate, and at other times we will adopt a more academic tone. The book expresses our desire to bring a tone of more intellectual inquiry into teachers' cultures, while at the same time cultivating theory to give it more of a practical and applied dimension.

This introduction has been relatively abstract, but teachers do not experience alienated teaching as a disembodied idea. On the contrary, alienated teaching manifests itself as an intense lived experience. To illustrate this phenomenon, Chapter 1 provides a case study of an urban teacher in the midst of change. Chapter 2, entitled "Growing into Mindful Teaching," describes the origins of our Mindful Teacher seminars and their theoretical location at the nexus of research on teacher inquiry, Ellen Langer's cognitive approach to mindfulness, and the engaged Buddhism of Thich Nhat Hanh. In Chapter 3 we enter into the heart of the Mindful Teacher seminars, describing the eightfold structure we used to explore the topic and ten clusters of questions teachers generated in the seminar setting. Six anchoring illustrations of teachers who engage in mindful reflection on their work convey the many challenges teachers have to work with today, as well as the resolutions that they found to meet specific difficulties.

Chapter 4 then develops a theoretical superstructure from the dynamics that emerged in the Mindful Teacher seminar setting. We identify and describe seven synergies of mindful teaching—interrelated values and strategies that classroom teachers can use on a daily basis to integrate more reflection and attunement into their busy work lives. Because no set of formulas can ever resolve all of the complexities that emerge in a given classroom, we then articulate what we call the triple tensions of mindful teaching—contradictions that are embedded in the teaching relationship itself and that only briefly can be overcome as part of a dynamic process that unfolds over time.

Finally, in Chapter 5 we turn to the theme of mindful teacher leadership. If teachers are to overcome alienated teaching, this most likely will not unfold as a solitary act, but rather as a result of a series of nested activities that will require leadership from teachers themselves. Mindful teacher leadership requires careful calibration because the lure of leadership, if not modulated and checked, can lead teachers *away from* rather than *into* the heart of teaching and learning (Ogilby, 2007). To avoid such goal displacement, we conceptualize three domains of micro-, meso-, and macrolevel changes, and invite teachers to raise their professional engagement to new and inspiring dimensions even as they remain committed to and engaged with the students they teach to and learn from on a daily basis.

CHAPTER 1

The Great Divide

LIZ MACDONALD: AUTOBIOGRAPHICAL REFLECTIONS

L IKE MANY INDIVIDUALS who find their way to teaching, as an undergraduate majoring in political science I never planned on becoming an elementary school teacher. However, when I moved home in the fall of 1995, I found myself in need of a job. Therefore I decided to sub in the Boston Public Schools (BPS). By late fall my subbing at different schools evolved into a long-term substitute position in a first-grade inclusion classroom. I didn't know the first thing about teaching, but things seemed to fall into place based on some natural intuition, endless hours of reading through teacher manuals, and the support of outstanding teacher colleagues.

Charlotte Haley and Ellen Murphy, different in their approaches, but both exceptional and creative first-grade teachers, took me by the hand and walked me through first grade. At the time I didn't care whether they were whole-language or phonics people, Black or White, teaching explicitly or implicitly, or constructivists or into direct instruction. I just needed ways to teach children! Both women modeled dedication to children, and their cultures and were incredibly supportive of me when the urban teaching experience would begin to overwhelm me. In retrospect, I'm pretty sure that I might well have left teaching were it not for their affirmations of my potential, their advice on complicated matters regarding communications with parents, and their unyielding belief in the potential of their students. They continually inspired me, and I thank them from the bottom of my heart.

What originally was simply a stop-gap measure to buy time to think about my next career steps, quickly became an all-consuming passion. Working with children day after day was incredibly satisfying and brought me an endless supply of joy. I was learning so much from the children, including their rich cultural and linguistic diversity and the communities in which they lived. I was impressed when I learned that more than half of my students were bilingual, speaking both their native language and English. There were several occasions when I was invited into the homes of my students for dinner during which I experienced the warmth and hospitality of parents, siblings, and often extended family members. Due to busing in the district, many of my students were living in different sections of the city, and as I visited their homes or their after-school programs, I would find myself discovering tight-knit communities I had never known in the city. My ignorance of urban children and their environments slowly was transforming into knowledge of a variety of languages, cultures, and family structures.

At the same time, there were some exasperating discoveries, including the fact that even though district mandates required the school to have a full-time aide in my inclusion classroom, no such aide was forthcoming in the cash-strapped district. This was the case even though I had one student with severe infant fetal alcohol syndrome who regularly wandered out of my class and generally operated with the cognitive abilities of a 3-year-old. I discovered that one mother of a child in my class was being beaten by her husband, a professional who worked at a local university; I then helped the mother and her child to enter a women's shelter. I wondered why one boy was a perpetual torment to other children in class, but upon driving him to his after-school "program," I was stunned to drop him off in a crowded tenement with roughly 15 children in it and one healthcare "provider" who spoke only Spanish (while the boy spoke only English).

Highly motivated to continue and improve my teaching, I subsequently entered a masters program and became certified in elementary education. I was completely immersed in teaching at this point. I would meet with literacy coaches at coffee shops on weekends; I spent hours shopping for materials in teacher resource stores; and I attended as many workshops as I could.

I had learned and was practicing every new teaching strategy I could get my hands on and I felt that things looked the way that they should in my classroom. Still, I wasn't confident that my students were learning at an appropriate rate. Nonetheless, I did feel validated in 1999, when I was honored as one of five district teachers who received a Resident Teacher Award for exemplary practices.

Outside of my BPS world, I began engaging in community organizing projects with grass-roots organizations in Boston and developed professional development workshops on literacy in collaboration with the Massachusetts Department of Education that exposed me to a wide range of educators and policy makers throughout the northeast. I continued to attend conferences and to collaborate with all kinds of instructors and specialists, and especially with colleagues at the Lynch School of Education at Boston College. I found myself evolving into a new role—that of a teacher leader.

By the spring of 2006 I became increasingly aware of contradictions in my life as an educator. Since 1999 I had mentored student teachers from Boston College in my classroom and since 2001 I had taught sections of undergraduate and graduate teacher preparatory classes there. As a lecturer at Boston College, I encouraged teacher candidates to explore a full range of diverse instructional practices in their teaching. Ironically, however, in my own fourth-grade classroom I found that my teaching was not promoting the learning gains for which I had hoped. As a teacher at the higher education level I felt idealistic and I could tell that many student teachers looked up to me—but in my own classroom I questioned my abilities and was painfully aware of the slow progress some of my students were making. To a certain extent, I felt more anguish than I had felt in my first year of teaching, because now I knew so much more—but was still unable to translate that knowledge into pupil learning gains. All too often I found myself at my wits' end, especially when working with several pupils who were learning, but at a slower pace than the policymakers who created the Massachusetts Comprehensive Assessment System (MCAS) test would have found acceptable.

My experience of the disconnect between my efficacy in the higher education classroom and my struggles in my elementary school led to me to a series of extended dialogues with colleagues at both the university and primary levels. Why was it that I felt I could teach others how to teach, but was so challenged in my own classroom? Upon further investigation, I came to discover that on several occasions I was engaging in classroom practices not because I thought that they were best for my pupils, but rather because I thought that they were what I was supposed to do. I was acquiescing in teaching practices that felt artificial to me, and I did so primarily out of a sense of deference to the district. Upon reflection, I observed that pupil misbehavior was greatest when I was using practices that I believed in least.

What kinds of district-mandated practices had I adopted? Ironically, most of them were drawn from the repertoire of child-centered, inquiry-driven practices that I believed in and that I promoted in my teacher education classes. The BPS mandated the use of Readers and Writers Workshop (http://www.readersandwritersworkshop.com) and TERC mathematics (http://www2.terc.edu/), both constructivist approaches to curriculum and instruction. The district required elementary school teachers to provide instruction and affiliated activities for 2 hours a day in the language arts and 70 minutes a day in mathematics. Significantly, it was not so much the actual *content of these practices* as it was the *nature of their implementation* that appeared to create difficulties.

My experiences in this regard are supported by scholars who have researched the impact of mandated changes on teachers (Bailey, 2000; Cohen, 1990; Hargreaves, 2004). According to this research, one of the major problems of educational change occurs when teachers are asked to shift from one instructional approach to another without adequate support. When I first began teaching in Boston, my school used a Houghton Mifflin basal reading anthology and the John Collins Writing Folder program. The latter dictated what genres the students should be writing in, along with what specific writing skills should be taught. I didn't like this highly structured program because my students rarely had the opportunity to write about subjects that interested them.

Under the leadership of Superintendent Thomas Payzant, the BPS subsequently abolished both the basal readers and the writing folders and implemented the Readers and Writers Workshop. Embedded in the Workshop's philosophy is the tenet that students need to have choices over what they write and that their writing should be modeled after published writers' work using "mentor texts." I was among the first cohort of teachers in the district to receive professional development in the Workshop model. Even though I had many questions about the model, I began implementation in my fourth-grade classroom before the mandate was implemented in my school.

I was pleased to discover that my own pedagogy of teaching writing mirrored much of what I understood the Writers Workshop to advocate. I believed that students needed choices, that they could learn through examples of good writing, and that their writing should be taken from one stage to the next through individual conferencing. However, the lack of accompanying materials, other than mentor texts, and the absence of a curriculum guide, left me somewhat uncertain as to what to teach and when.

Following the structure of the Workshop model, I taught 15-minute mini-lessons, allowed the students to write in their notebooks for 35 minutes, and subsequently had the whole class discuss their writing for the last 10 minutes. Having no specified curriculum other than the state standards, I struggled to plan mini-lessons each day. Since a majority of my students performed below grade level and many were English language learners, writing for 35 minutes without interruption was a major challenge for them. Some students began doodling, others distracted one another by poking or prodding their neighbors, and some simply wrote lyrics from rap songs over and over again. I found that conferencing regularly with each student—as is called for by the Writers Workshop—was an enormous challenge because so many students were easily distracted when I was focused on a single student.

I experienced similar difficulties with math reforms. In an attempt to implement TERC mathematics systematically districtwide, the school system's math department created a pacing guide outlining which investigations (lessons) should be taught each day at each grade level throughout the district. A district mandate sought to ensure consistency and continuity in math instruction across schools. TERC is a spiral curriculum, weaving mathematical concepts in each unit of study throughout the year, and building upon concepts and strategies introduced at previous grade levels. Theoretically, full implementation of the program is essential to its success.

Like many of my colleagues, I found that it was a challenge to keep up with the pacing guide's schedule. Like me, other teachers in the district encountered students every day whose conceptual understanding and basic mathematical skills were so limited that more time needed to be spent with a single investigation. For example, an investigation might require pupils to solve a complex multiplication word story. When my students tried to solve such problems, I often discovered that they not only lacked proficiency in multiplication facts, but had a weak understanding of the concept of multiplication itself. At these junctures I knew that my pupils needed additional time to learn about multiplication, but the pacing guide made it difficult to take the time to remediate my struggling learners. In such instances, I usually chose to follow the pacing guide rather than dig down deeper into content, in part because my pupils were tested every 4 to 6 weeks. I believe that the times when I made that decision to follow the pacing guide coincided with a rise in students' behavioral difficulties and their learning was at its lowest level.

Research shows that the best-intentioned and most research-grounded of reforms often break down at the level of implementation (Cohen, 1990; McLaughlin, 2006; Pressman & Wildavsky, 1973). When I presented these obstacles of teaching and learning to coaches in my district, I felt that I did not receive assistance, but simply was met with the assertion that I needed to find a way to make the Workshop model successful. I felt that I was at fault. It was as if there were no flaws in the Workshop itself, but only in my delivery of instruction and my organization of the classroom. This sense of failure was especially exasperating to me because I had welcomed the Readers and Writers Workshop as a creative alternative to the John Collins Writing Folder. Questioning my abilities as a teacher, I continued using the Readers and Writers Workshop despite my intuition that I was not providing optimal instruction for my students.

Like many other teachers, I really made a good-faith effort to implement my school district's curriculum and to comply with mandated reforms. I always was on the lookout for new resources to incorporate into my lessons throughout the year. Some of those resources took me far away from the Readers and Writers Workshop approach. For example, I found that some familiarity with systematic phonics provided me with a broader repertoire of teaching practices that benefited some of my struggling readers and writers. I learned that there were many sides to the literacy wars, that it went against my nature to choose one side and enter into battle with the others, and that I wanted to remain open to and inclusive of the full array of instructional approaches that different reformers advocated.

What kinds of instructional practices did I want to use? In addition to my role as a facilitator of pupils' knowledge construction, as advocated by Readers and Writers Workshop and TERC, I wanted to take advantage of a wide range of practices that would allow me to share my own zest for continual learning and my enthusiasm for literature and mathematics with my pupils. I felt that I needed more structure in terms of using the Readers and Writers Workshop and wanted to know that I was covering all of the reading skills that my children needed. I wanted children to learn several ways of conceptualizing mathematics problems, but I also wanted to make sure that they were comfortable with a certain amount of memorization in mathematics so that they were prepared for state tests when they needed to recall information about multiplication tables at a moment's notice. While I liked the emphasis on children thinking for themselves and in small groups, I believed that these activities needed to be supplemented with well-designed, teacher-led instruction to make sure that the children had new knowledge on which to scaffold their extended learning activities.

These critical reflections then led me to question many aspects of the culture of urban educational reform today. Can teaching ever be excellent when teachers use practices that we believe are of limited value to children? What kinds of cultural spaces are available to teachers to share our misgivings about instructional programs, or to adopt them selectively into our pre-existing repertoire of practices? Are students able to detect when teachers are using practices that we ourselves are skeptical about?

CONCEPTUALIZING ALIENATED TEACHING

Derived from the sociological theory of "alienated labor" (Marx, 1844/1978), alienated teaching is intended to describe instructional processes in which teachers neglect teaching practices that they believe are best suited for their pupils and instead comply with externally imposed mandates out of a sense of deference to authority. Research indicates that teachers' compliance comes at a considerable cost, as teachers' loss of professional autonomy and agency can lead to low morale, a loss of self-efficacy, and disinvestment from teaching (Bailey, 2000; Craig, 2006; Hargreaves, 2002, 2003). Alienated teaching would appear to be especially problematic because of the emotionally charged nature of teaching and learning (Fried, 1995; Hargreaves, 1994; Nieto, 2003).

One could well imagine multiple routes in responding to the instructional dilemmas described above. For example, there is the strategy of protest. In this scenario, one dissents from the district's mandates and argues against the erosion of teacher autonomy. Such protest typically comes at a high cost to teachers, for while they might not actually be fired for failing to comply, they can suffer loss of professional opportunities and status as a result of public disagreement with district reforms.

A second strategy would be loyalty. One recognizes that teachers are not high up in the hierarchy of urban school systems; accommodates new mandates the best one can, casting off previous practices with regret but not dwelling on them; and aligns one's instruction as neatly as possible to new standards and practices. One "goes along to get along," avoids catastrophizing on the basis of unfortunate aspects of reforms, and capitalizes on the positive aspects to the best of one's abilities.

In a third option, one can go underground, so to speak, shutting the door and carrying on a quiet, surreptitious revolt as a lone rebel. Part of this strategy can entail waiting until a new superintendent comes, anticipating that the pedagogical pendulum will swing back in one's direction with enough patience and a touch of luck. This option of privatized teaching is popular, perhaps even widespread, with many veteran teachers, who have tired of the perpetual merry-go-round of reform initiatives and prefer simply to hone their craft in the solitude of the cellular classroom.

Finally, a fourth option involves exit. Nationally, over 50% of beginning teachers in urban school systems exercise this route in their first 3 years of teaching. The ability to exercise professional autonomy is the most important criterion in teachers' job satisfaction (Ingersoll, 2003). When beginning teachers experience that such autonomy is not to be a part of their professional identity, they typically seek employment elsewhere.

LIZ MACDONALD: CONTINUED REFLECTIONS

In my case, my response to these dilemmas was complicated. As a general principle, I endorsed the open-ended approaches of the Readers and Writers Workshop and constructivist mathematics mandated by the

BPS. I felt fortunate to work in a district where the cultivation of children's abilities as independent thinkers and problem solvers was at the center of school improvement efforts. Furthermore, I had begun an exciting collaboration with Professor Maria Estela Brisk of Boston College on teaching English language learners, resulting in my first academic publication (Brisk et al., 2002). I was not interested in demonizing the school system, which I believed was led by many conscientious individuals who genuinely had the children's best interests at heart. Hence, the stance of protest did not seem to me especially valuable, because I found much that was praiseworthy in the reforms that privileged Readers and Writers Workshop and TERC investigations. Rather, it was their externally mandated nature and lack of high-quality, ongoing support that was problematic. I had no desire to exit urban schools or teaching altogether; I did not wish to conceal my teaching practices by shutting my classroom doors; and I wanted to be as public and open in my philosophy and practices of education as possible.

In the summer of 2005 I conducted professional development workshops for urban teachers as part of a consultancy with the Massachusetts Department of Education. While working with other classroom teachers, I learned that many other educators shared my experience of alienated teaching. Teachers would ask me questions about how much freedom they had to stray from the selected reading program in order to modify and supplement the curriculum to meet the needs of their students, worrying that they might go too far and get in trouble with their principal or superintendent. Many teachers appeared fearful of district reprisals if they departed from prescribed pedagogical strategies or curricula, even if the supplementary materials had many intrinsic merits and might appeal especially to diverse pupils in urban environments. Some teachers reported that school officials locked away their old curricula when new ones arrived so that teachers would be allowed to use only the new program's materials. At one low-performing school in the state, a teacher informed me that she stopped a common reading practice in her classroom because a publishing company representative told her it did not fit into the company's program. When I asked the teacher whether she thought that previous practice was beneficial, she replied that it had indeed benefited her pupils—and she didn't know why she had given it up. These conversations led me to recognize how fragile teacher professionalism is today, and how needful teachers are of continual support and guidance from their colleagues, administrators, and the public in general.

To deal with these challenges, I sought ideas, dialogues, and resources that could help me with the dilemma of alienated teaching. I wanted to avoid a polarizing, simplistic debate that would pit me as a classroom teacher against my urban public school system. I knew that the the district was stretched thin by budget crises, often reflected rather than manufactured larger social inequalities, and was in need of teacher leadership in buildings throughout the district. Yet where could I turn for support?

By the spring of 2005 I was at a breaking point in my instruction. Even though I had taught for 10 years in the BPS, had won professional accolades, and was a widely recognized teacher leader, in my own fourth-grade classroom I was all too aware of my frailties and shortcomings. I found myself preoccupied by one boy with a severe case of ADHD who could turn the best-planned lesson into chaos for the whole class; by a girl who was struggling with her math and cried daily because she was fearful of not being promoted along with her cohort; by several students who I knew were highly capable but simply did not appear motivated enough to devote themselves to their academic achievement. I was exerting a tremendous amount of energy in my teaching and spending hours outside of the school day planning to make things right. I felt like I was running up Heartbreak Hill and the peak was nowhere in sight.

THE IMPORTANCE OF FEDERAL LEADERSHIP

How can one recognize when one is falling into patterns of alienated teaching and imbuing remote policy makers with more control of one's daily interactions with children than they deserve? And how can one keep good teachers in the classroom, not out of masochistic self-abnegation, but out of genuine love of children, and joy and fulfillment in meeting real educational needs?

As indicated above, we have no silver bullets to shoot into the educational policy arena. We believe that being a good teacher is extraordinarily demanding work, and that if one really cares about one's teaching, one perpetually is reinventing lessons, hunting out new materials to engage disaffected pupils, and learning from colleagues and from research about new ways to modify curricula and group activities. All of this tinkering is the heart and soul of teachers' daily practice, and making sure that good teachers possess the tools and cultural settings in which they can flourish is the responsibility of educational leaders, policy makers, and the public at large.

Good teaching will always be hard, and it will always be harder in environments that are underresourced and that suffer from long-standing social inequities. There will always be complicated pupils, intrusive parents, and controlling administrators. The more that one promotes simplified agendas to solve all of these prosaic problems of everyday life, the more that one raises false expectations and contributes to the air of unreality and fads that shapes far too many educational contexts.

As one settles into teaching as a career and begins to realize that an educational utopia really isn't right around the corner, the realization comes that one is going to need to pace oneself and find certain ways to build regular networks of support into one's work routines. In our case, we first began collaborating on a Title II Teacher Quality Enhancement (TQE) grant funded by the U.S. Department of Education that promoted school and university collaborations. The TQE grants were an extraordinary example of federal leadership, funded in the last full year (1999) of the Clinton administration, that provided funding to restructure colleges and university-based teacher education programs in order to encourage experimental partnerships to support urban schools. Our particular grant linked 7 colleges and universities—Boston College, the University of Massachusetts at Amherst, the University of Massachusetts at Boston, Clark University, Lesley University, Northeastern University, and Wheelock College—with 18 urban schools in Boston, Springfield, and Worcester. Significantly, the grant provided our "Massachusetts Coalition for Teacher Quality and Student Achievement" with $7.2 million of funding spread over 6 years.

With support from the grant, we began team-teaching across our school and university boundaries to learn more about each other's challenges and to embed teacher preparatory activities in real urban school environments (Shirley, 2006a, 2006b; Shirley et al., 2006). We came to know each other and many of each other's colleagues through the federal funding, which provided us with badly needed resources to host summer conferences for extended learning opportunities about challenges and opportunities in urban schools and communities. Along with our other school and university colleagues, we attended conferences and presented our work at symposia sponsored by Urban Networks to Improve Teacher Education, the Holmes Partnership, and the annual meetings of the American Educational Research Association. These joint activities, shared with many others, allowed us to build trust and confidence in one another and to persevere in overcoming the "great divide" between school and university faculty.

While on the one hand funding from Title II represented an unprecedented opportunity to support school and university partnerships, it also raised sensitive turf issues of control and power both within and across institutional settings. Why is it that so few teacher education courses in higher education institutions are offered in collaboration with experienced urban teachers? Why is it that colleges and universities can skim off huge amounts of money in "overhead" expenses related to running grant-funded projects? What happens when budget cutbacks in a system like the BPS threaten to destroy carefully nourished partnership activities, and higher education institutions are left absorbing what originally were planned to be shared expenditures? And how can the fragile human relationships that are built across institutional lines by "boundary spanners" be preserved when upper-level administrators undermine partnerships by following protocols rigidly rather than bending rules to serve the larger public good?

When we first began team-teaching in September 2001, we realized that weekly meetings were going to be imperative, and after a couple of early forays panned out, we settled on Jim's Deli, a bustling restaurant a couple of miles away from the Garfield Elementary School. We found this deli—owned by an immigrant Greek family, with Jim himself providing local color by shunning long trousers in favor of shorts even in the fiercest Boston weather—to be the perfect setting in which to enjoy steaming hot coffee, sizzling French toast, and a side order of sunnyside-up eggs. For 8 years now we have been regular customers at Jim's, and have used his deli as a home base to meet with other teachers, community organizers, and visitors from out of town who want to learn more about school and university partnerships. It was at Jim's where we first concocted the idea of a "mindful teacher project" that we hoped would help us to transcend the educational limitations and cultures of both of our respective institutional settings, and which is described more fully in the next chapter.

CHAPTER 2

Growing Into Mindful Teaching

ONE MIGHT ASK at this juncture something along the following lines: "What's the big deal? New policies are always coming along. Educators are professionals, so one should always use one's professional discretion; it's one's right. Liz, take what you want from the Readers and Writers' Workshop and TERC investigations and ignore the rest. Don't get bogged down in literal interpretations of new mandates."

How easy it sounds! This (only apparently wise) advice ignores the high-pressure educational policy context of recent years. David Hopkins (2001), a leading school improvement thinker in the United Kingdom, has described the "policy epidemic" (p. 4) that is sweeping developed nations, in which legislators have placed upon school systems enormous expectations, which vastly exceed their capacity, to rectify long-standing social injustices. This "pathology of central policy change" (p. 4) has created anxiety and guilt for conscientious educators, who burn the midnight oil trying to find research that will help them to pump up their test scores an extra notch in search of adequate yearly progress.

Yet just when one might seek to stigmatize policy makers as witless Gradgrinds of educational change, we would rather argue the opposite: that one must give credit for the innovative and even emancipatory dimensions of some policy reforms. The Title II grants that funded the Massachusetts Coalition, for example, gave us valuable resources from which we could learn about the modalities of educational change in the three largest urban school districts in Massachusetts, could organize workshops and annual summer institutes with student and teacher participation from urban high schools, and could encourage reticent faculty in both the urban public school and the higher education faculty to venture into one another's classrooms to develop a variety of innovative and engaging learning activities.

These diverse experiences with colleagues from around the state were enormously broadening and helped us to traverse the limitations of our respective school and higher education settings. In a very real way, an entity like the Massachusetts Coalition represented an enactment of John Dewey's (1916) philosophy of democratic education, which hinged upon drawing together diverse constituencies and enabling them to identify common interests to promote the public good. Although we had not yet come up with the term "alienated teaching" at the time, we knew that something was wrong with most mainstream reform movements and that we wanted to find a way of addressing it. Unfortunately, most grant-funded activities require applicants to endorse the funders' assumptions as the point of departure and provide little flexibility for a classroom teacher and professor to develop their own agenda.

Our own situation provided a happy exception in this regard. For years the BPS and Boston College had collaborated in mutual activities, and this collegiality had become institutionalized in the form of "Boston Collaborative Fellows" grants that were administered by Boston College and the Boston Public Schools collectively. We applied for and received a grant to launch a "mindful teacher" project that would provide us with stipends for cohorts of Boston public school teachers who would be willing to join us in a seminar structure entailing common readings, reflection on teaching practices, journal entries, classroom visits, an on-line chat room, and a research project. The seminars would be designed to provide participants with opportunities to reflect upon their teaching, to discuss ongoing curricular reforms in the BPS, to learn about new teaching strategies, and to do so in a collegial setting. Above all, we wanted to get past the perpetual merry-go-round of fads and innovations to explore a deeper side of education, should it be accessible to us.

Yet identifying many of the problems of educational change hardly is the same thing as coming up with sensible alternatives. To begin to move in this direction, we consulted three separate intellectual streams of thought.

PROFESSIONAL LEARNING COMMUNITIES

First, we explored the large body of research on teacher inquiry as enacted in what many scholars describe as "professional learning communities" (Stoll & Louis, 2007). Recall that many years ago Dan Lortie (1975) described teachers' microcultures as trapped in a vicious circle of individualism, conservatism, and presentism. Although there is variation in the outcomes data, it appears that when successfully organized and led, professional learning communities provide invaluable levers for teachers by helping them to break out of their isolation and provide emotional support for one another, swap lesson plans and share information about pupils, and to develop kinds of distributed leadership that make the decisive difference between a "learning enriched" and a "learning impoverished" environment (Rosenholtz, 1989).

Reviewing the literature on professional learning communities, we found a number of similarities among scholars and practitioners, with a variety of different emphases in terms of research methodologies and policy recommendations. In one of the most well-known variants, Donald Schön (1987) popularized the notion of the "reflective practitioner" who goes beyond a direct assimilation of information to conceptualize one's work in a creative manner that can circumvent established protocols to develop more powerful and efficacious ways of meeting one's goals. Patricia King and Karen Strohm Kitchener (1994) developed a model of "reflective judgment" that had more empirical foundations than Schön's work and encouraged the development of critical thinking and informed professional autonomy. These works have important European analogues in what some have described as the "German tradition of didactic analysis" that has been a foundational part of teacher education in Europe for decades (Shirley, 2008a, 2008b; Westbury, Hopmann, & Riquarts, 2000).

Much of the literature on teacher inquiry and teacher leadership incorporates notions of collaborative reflection, discussion, evaluation, and action (Blankstein, Houston, & Cole, 2008). A number of these notions have important affinities with Paolo Freire's (2000) concept of the "generative theme" (p. 97) that is elaborated by teacher-researchers from a process of collaborative inquiry with a "cultural circle" of adult learners, although they typically do not engage the political dimensions of teaching and learning as deliberately as Freire did. While there are various scholarly debates on reflective practice and teacher inquiry (Liston & Zeichner, 1990; Selman, 1988), the debates share a number of common assumptions. For example, the authors all value the here-and-now and almost prosaic everyday quality of classroom interaction. The authors all emphasize the need for teachers perpetually to question their assumptions about teaching and learning in the light of new findings about their pupils. Likewise, they all view teaching as a genuinely intellectual activity in which even the smallest choices contain ethical and political dimensions that call forth the highest kinds of reflection and judgment.

Sonia Nieto, for example, has a section in her enormously popular and teacher-friendly book *What Keeps Teachers Going?* (2003) entitled "Obsessed by Mindful Teaching" (pp. 88–89). In that section she describes Stephen Gordon, an accomplished Boston public school teacher who expressed an anguished confusion about the best way to reach his urban pupils. In Nieto's account, accepting the raw emotional vulnerability of teaching, and learning to share that with others, can help one to penetrate to the core meaning of teaching as a vocation. In this interpretation, mindfulness requires a full engagement with the existential complexity of teaching in all of its emotional, interpersonal, and even spiritual plenitude.

As professional learning communities (PLCs)have proliferated, some researchers (Hargreaves & Shirley, 2009b) have raised concerns that some PLCs have become subtly coercive, so that rather than providing teachers with genuine opportunities for probing deeply into issues of teaching and learning, they instead have become thinly veiled venues for staging "contrived collegiality" (Hargreaves, 1994, p. 186). Others (Murrell, 1998; Noguera, 2008; Payne, 2008) have cautioned that PLCs in too many cases have become narrowly technical in their orientations and have marginalized important discussions of race, ethnicity, and student and community cultures from their deliberations. With much of the recent drive for raising academic achievement, it appears that PLCs in too many settings have developed an exclusive focus on data-driven decision making, so that other ways of conceptualizing teachers' reflective inquiry have been marginalized and discredited. In these instances teachers have become "data-driven to distraction" (Shirley & Hargreaves, 2006). While we cannot comment on how widespread such distortions may have become, we do know that in launching the Mindful Teacher project we very much wanted to avoid such predetermined and limiting constraints.

ELLEN LANGER'S STUDIES OF MINDFULNESS

Second, we were drawn to the research of Harvard psychologist Ellen Langer, who in her studies on mindfulness, offered a triple definition that focused on the juxtaposition of cognition to habit. For Langer (1997), mindfulness entails "the continuous creation of new categories; openness to new information; and an implicit awareness of more than one perspective" (p. 4). She contrasts mindfulness with "mindlessness," which she characterizes as "entrapment in old categories; by automatic behavior that precludes attending to new signals; and by action that operates from a single perspective" (p. 4). In her experiments, Langer developed a variety of what she termed "mindfulness treatments" and documented how they advanced powerful new ways of thinking and acting. Langer's approach was appealing to us because of its empiricism; her witty, zestful style as an author; and her special interest in "mindful learning," which spoke well to our interests in diverse and creative instructional modalities. This form of mindfulness did not entail any formal meditation practices and hence created an opening to the concept for those teachers unfamiliar with meditation.

ENGAGED BUDDHISM

Separate from these recent developments in the social sciences—and most challenging and discrepant for our future investigations—mindfulness is a central concept in Buddhism. Classic Buddhist sutras, such as the Heart Sutra and the Diamond Sutra, articulate notions of mindfulness that encourage sensitivity to the here-and-now sensations of the moment, compassion for all living beings, and ethical maxims for proper conduct (Hanh, 1988, 1992). Thich Nhat Hanh (1998) has elaborated 14 different "mindfulness trainings" (www.mindfulnessbell.org/14trainings.htm) that are intended to encourage detachment from one's own views (so as to be open to others), moderation in one's consumption (so as to share prosperity with the less fortunate and preserve the earth's resources), and compassion (given the prevalence of human suffering). Hanh's own courage in protesting the war in Vietnam as a young man and living for over 40 years in exile in France, as well as his unwavering commitment to nonviolence and social justice, seemed especially attractive to us given our social justice commitments as urban educators—as well as an important refutation of the fear that mindful contemplation might entail political passivity or apathy. Of direct relevance to education, Robert Tremmel (1993) has shown that aspects of the Buddhist understanding of mindfulness can be infused into teacher inquiry activities to reduce teachers' presuppositions about their pupils, to attend more fully to pupils' actual learning processes, and to track and modify their emotional responses to classroom interactions.

Reference to Buddhism, of course, is highly unorthodox in professional learning communities and mainstream educational change. We are not Buddhists and we see no empirical evidence that would support traditional Eastern tenets such as reincarnation. At the same time, we also have taken note of the growing quantity of empirical research (Austin, 1998; Siegel, 2007; Wallace, 2003) confirming that certain Buddhist practices, such as mindfulness meditation, carry numerous psychological benefits, including the ability to apprehend new forms of information without excessive ideological filtering. One of us has participated regularly in a *sangha* or meditation community in the tradition of engaged Buddhism since 2000. We wanted to build meditation into our theory of action, not as a panacea, but as an additional resource to help teachers to detach themselves from and gain more critical insight into the broader educational context in which they are enmeshed.

AN INTEGRATIVE APPROACH

These three strands—teacher inquiry in professional learning communities, Langer's mindfulness research, and Thich Nhat Hanh's engaged Buddhism—provided conceptual underpinnings of "mindful teaching" that we have brought to our Mindful Teacher seminars. Yet our enactment of ideas from these three strands is very much our own ensemble of activities and values. Without disrespecting the enormous intellectual and spiritual contributions from each of the three strands, and especially from the 2,500-year-old tradition of Buddhism, our goal was not so much to master their respective bodies of knowledge as it was to appropriate them, almost with a light touch, to enable us to better understand our interactions with our children and colleagues in our own classrooms and schools. We studied tenets of Buddhism, such as the Noble Eightfold Path, not to memorize them, but to enable us to practice detachment from views and to examine our teaching through another set of lenses with a high moral purpose.

This careful exploratory approach in and of itself seemed in accord with Thich Nhat Hanh's writings. In his book *Keeping the Peace: Mindfulness and Public Service* (2005), he wrote, "Don't think that you have to 'be a Buddhist' or understand everything about mindfulness right away" (p. 12). Our goal was to take some tentative first steps and to integrate mindfulness practices into our everyday lives. Without this, mindfulness meditation could become another dogma that one tries on and discards just like so many other fashions and trends. Here we draw upon the insight that knowledge in itself can be an obstacle to further learning if it leads to "rubricizing" (Maslow, 1969, p. 81) or the imposition of classificatory schemes upon reality in ways that obscure rather than enhance new growth.

This, then, is the kernel of our understanding of mindful teaching in the contemporary educational context. It entails recognizing that in spite of the push for standards, accountability, alignment, and DDDM, an alternate reality has emerged full of contradictions, messiness, and "human, all-too-human" problems. Yet with this acknowledgment come splendid opportunities to advance real learning—not just test-prep, or "gaming the system," or the kind of "reform" that cuts out recess in the name of academic rigor while children experience an obesity epidemic that can rob them of joyful childhoods and shorten their life expectancy. Our contention is that education can really improve only when teachers themselves have opportunities to become more reflective of the multiple pressures upon them and collaborate to build professional learning communities that promote deep and sustained thinking and analysis about the many problems in schools, and especially those in urban settings. Reformers often want teachers all to "be on the same page" and to "get everyone on board," but the reality is that educators have very different, and sometimes opposing, philosophies of education that often originate in their different life experiences.

Educators need activity settings in which to explore those differences and to discern both their benefits as well as their potential costs. Rather than suppressing their differences, teachers need ways of bringing them to light, discussing their strengths and potential weaknesses, and making them pedagogically generative. Mindful teaching will always entail openness to new information, a willingness to explore topics that are marginalized in the dominant reform fads of the moment, and a readiness to review one's previous assumptions as part of a life-long career marked by critical inquiry, reflection, and compassion.

THE PROFESSIONAL STAKES FOR TEACHERS

If mindful teaching occurs at the nexus of policy and instruction, then mindful teaching has an import that goes far beyond the simple adjustment of a teaching strategy here and a curriculum supplement there. At stake far more in these considerations is the very professional identity of teachers. We are working explicitly with an understanding of teaching that acknowledges (and yes, even cherishes) its tentative, experimental, iterative nature. We have tried enough different varieties of frontal instruction, small-group instruction, individualized curricula, and alternative forms of assessment to appreciate that every approach has both strengths and weaknesses. We have observed enough teachers to have learned just how personal and customized teaching needs to be, and how new practices simply cannot be plopped down onto pre-existing routines and values without a process of complex mutual adjustment between a teacher and a new program over time. Our contention is that teachers' professionalism relies on our ability to see multiple sides of the decisions that we make and to make informed judgments about which tools to use to provide the best instruction possible.

Accepting this open-endedness of education allows us to view teachers' professional decision making not as a problem to be avoided through impulsive overreaction to test scores or uncritical compliance with mandates, but rather as *an intellectual field in and of itself*. We seek to preserve and expand this fragile domain of professional learning and action that is abrogated so easily when political reformers of whatever stripe—whether liberal, conservative, or radical—move too closely into the heart of teaching and learning.

Given the massive policy shifts of recent American education, we have found it easy to strike up a conversation with virtually every urban public school teacher we have met, both in Boston and across the country, around the concept of alienated teaching. Teachers know all too well the loss of locus of control and boundary invasion that occur when shifting policy agendas move into their instructional activities. It is important to note that many teachers do not have a language with which to describe alienated teaching. The dominant phrase is simply the laconic "burnout," which psychologizes what are in fact deeply social processes. Yet what occurs when we share the concept of mindful teaching with educators, and pilot contemplative practices intended to enhance mindfulness? How do teachers subsequently endeavor to adapt the instruction in their classroom and schools in light of literature and practices affiliated with mindfulness?

To answer these queries we now turn to the Mindful Teacher seminars themselves.

CHAPTER 3

Practicing Mindfully

THUS FAR WE have set up an opposition between *alienated* teaching—which is coercive, privatized, and resented—and *mindful* teaching—which is integrative, reflective, and deep. But it may not be so easy to move from one experience of teaching to the other, and our criticism of alienated teaching might be more easily stated than avoided. German philosopher of education Lothar Klingberg (1990) argued in his theory of "dialectical didactics" that there are always power asymmetries at work in education and that students and teachers, even if they might long for deeper and more authentic relationships, often cannot resist tendencies to objectify and to a certain extent instrumentalize one another. The tradition of Socratic dialogues has long held that a moment of alienation in the form of cognitive dissonance is crucial to get learners out of their comfort zone and open to new ideas. And we know from many years of experiments in groupwork in social change organizations that even when individuals have the best of intentions and the most emancipatory social justice goals, subtle differences in styles of communication—such as tone of voice, eye contact, and other forms of body language—have powerful influences in how groups evolve (Pallotta, 2004).

Of course, the Mindful Teacher seminars that we established had no magic potions to offer in regard to these seemingly intractable dilemmas. Nor did we promise to concoct such potions. Rather, we wanted to *befriend* the complex and the intractable, anticipating that perhaps if we changed our frame of reference, we might come to understand our own teaching and learning differently, and could convey that new understanding to children in rewarding ways.

To help you to understand how we endeavored to do this, and with what consequences and outcomes, we will now

- Describe the *eightfold structure* of the Mindful Teacher seminars;
- Identify *ten clusters of questions* engendered through seminar discussions;

- Provide *six anchoring illustrations* of how seminar participants demonstrated aspects of mindfulness to reconceptualize and improve their work as educators.

THE KNOT OF NEEDFULNESS: LIZ MACDONALD

As a teacher in the school district, I knew that the Boston Public Schools offered high-quality professional development in innovative reading, writing, and mathematics teaching practices, along with training for teachers in systematic intervention programs that were well recognized among special educators. More recently, the district was offering professional development around the hot topics of the achievement gap and cultural competency. All of this professional development was relevant and beneficial. Still, what the district was not adequately offering teachers was a place where they could be emotionally, intellectually, and professionally supported in a collegial setting. There were not many settings provided—other than perhaps the local pub of a school's neighborhood—where teachers were able to discuss the emotional demands of urban teaching. And more often than not these informal settings that teachers found outside of school in which to vent about the daily challenges of teaching tended to turn into complaining sessions rather than opportunities for real reflection or productive planning.

Working collaboratively with faculty at Boston College, I was able to experience the scholarly side of the education world. I was able to stay current with educational research and I had the opportunity to attend national and international conferences where I could network with teacher educators and renowned educational researchers. Yet I wasn't fully satisfied. I wanted my fellow teachers to be able to experience this world and have their sense of professionalism enhanced, even though I knew that there was still a slight disconnect between educational research and classroom practice and I realized that reading research and attending conferences would not be enough. Believing that urban school teachers needed a place to discuss the emotional wear and tear of the classroom, I felt we needed a new kind of setting—a new "zone of mediation" in the words of one scholar (Welner, 2001, p. 94)—where teachers could share the many different questions that arose in the course of their everyday classroom realities.

CREATING AND STRUCTURING
THE MINDFUL TEACHER SEMINARS

It's one thing to attempt to create a setting in which teachers can develop and seek to answer their questions—and quite another to have success in doing so. The resolution to the questions generated by teachers, we believed, could come only through testing our ideas out in practice and by attempting to establish a tone of open and respectful inquiry that provided enough structure and confidence that teachers would be able to move quickly and productively into topics that concerned them. In our experience, a few preliminary ingredients were essential in getting things off to a good start. First, we had a highly recognized teacher leader who was more than willing to discuss challenges in her own classroom. Second, we had a university-based scholar who would prepare readings and lead discussions on what research had to say about teachers' different concerns. Third, we had a neutral setting on the Boston College campus that provided a splendid physical locale for meetings. Finally, we had stipends for teachers, provided through the Boston Collaborative Fellows grant—to match and even surpass district funds for professional development.

We developed a series of Saturday "Mindful Teacher" seminars, in which we met to discuss readings, to practice formal meditation, and to explore topics of relevance and concern for the teachers. Here we wanted to provide participants with material for intellectual development, and to do so in such a way that they could make connections to their everyday lives as classroom teachers. We read Ellen Langer's *The Power of Mindful Learning* (1997), Sonia Nieto's *What Keeps Teachers Going?* (2003), Thich Nhat Hanh's "Fourteen Mindfulness Trainings" (1998), and Ann Lieberman and Lynne Miller's *Teacher Leadership* (2004). In addition, we purchased Jon Kabat-Zinn's meditation CDs (www.mindfulnesstapes.com) and encouraged the teachers to meditate on their own as part of a regular formal mindfulness practice.

The organization of our Mindful Teacher seminars followed a common pattern that varied based on the evolving group contexts. Participants would arrive on a Saturday morning on the Boston College campus and have coffee and muffins for a half hour, catching up with one another about recent events in their schools and in their lives. There always seemed to be plenty of details to keep abreast of—the latest on the district's new literacy or math curriculum, a check-in with a colleague about a troubled pupil we had discussed in a previous session, or a teacher who was in the midst of conflict with her principal about changes in her assignment for the upcoming school year. We deliberately decided to keep the size of the seminars small—never amounting to more than 15 participants at their largest—to encourage a climate of community and mutual trust. And we deliberately chose settings that were cozy and comfortable rather than institutional and imposing, so that the purpose of knowledge acquisition promoted by a university would not be supplanted by the more imposing and even intimidating aspects of higher education institutions.

Pressing Concerns

After establishing a tone of relaxed informality, we would use eight structures to guide our seminars. We often began with a discussion of *pressing concerns* that we anticipated were widely shared by the teachers. For example, in January 2007 contract negotiations between the district and the Boston Teachers Union appeared to have broken down, and after a long period in which teachers were on "work-to-rule" (in which the union tells members to abstain from any activities that are not specified in their contracts), teachers went out on picket lines and a strike was narrowly averted at the eleventh hour. Just a month later a rash of youth violence spiked in Boston, culminating in a student being shot on a city bus when returning home from school in the middle of the afternoon. These incidents provoked extended conversations on the various conflicting messages teachers received about the strike and the dangers facing young people growing up in the central city. On other occasions, more prosaic concerns, such as the district's initiation of collaborative coaching and learning by teacher leaders, provided topics that led to animated conversations.

Selective Vulnerability

Next, we moved into a preselected topic of *selective vulnerability* from a teacher leader on a question of immediate concern to that person. In some instances we knew that teachers were struggling with administrators about topics ranging from test preparation to curriculum implementation to simply the tone of voice used when issuing directives to staff. In other cases teachers brought forth issues that were entirely within their purview. One particularly lively session began with the question, "I've hidden the pencil sharpener—now what?" in which a teacher opened up for conversation the topic of compromises that we all make when trying to establish a peaceful classroom environment but simultaneously curtailing students' freedom of movement. On other occasions teachers discussed their exasperation at the many factors—from announcements over loudspeakers to disrespectful colleagues to entertaining but educationally useless school assemblies—that cut into their precious instructional time. In such instances the teachers found immediate entry to areas in which they also struggled and they shared strategies and responses that they found helpful with one another.

Scholarly Research

A third component of the Mindful Teacher seminars concerned a brief presentation and discussion of *scholarly research* on a topic. Here the effort was to expand teachers' awareness of their everyday concerns by informing them of what scholarship indicated on the matter. Our discussions differed from some policy briefs calling for "translational research" (Dynarski, 2008, p. 52) because we believe that scholarship on topics such as literacy instruction, math curricula, and second-language learning often is quite contested, sometimes vehemently so. Yet teachers often are told that "research proves that . . ." as if research findings are clear and the consequences for implementation are unambiguous. When teachers receive such messages, their own diverse and contradictory experiences are rendered suspect. Teachers need to know that scholarship provides clear answers to their questions in some areas—inconsistent messages around classroom management are commonly disastrous, for example—but ambiguous findings in others—a blending of phonics and whole language is recommended by most reading experts, for example, but the nature of the blending is open to interpretation (Snow, Burns, & Griffin, 1998). Hence, there is no bypassing the need for careful discernment of complex issues and the continual honing of reflective judgment that is *informed* but not *driven* by available research.

Formal Meditation

Fourth, as a regular part of seminar activities, we practiced *formal meditation* to calm and concentrate the mind. Most of our participants had received no formal meditation trainings previously, and while they were curious about meditation, it is of course highly unorthodox for teachers to sit silently together with their eyes closed or focused on a mid-range object a few feet away from them! Yet once the teachers settled into the idea that meditation was not part of a cult and the seminar leaders had no covert agenda of proselytizing, they generally came to cherish this time for peace, quiet, and focused contemplation.

There are of course many different forms of meditation. In one form, individuals simply try to clear and calm their minds, for example, by following their breath and continually returning to the breath when they find themselves drifting away with preoccupations. Here it is a matter of acknowledging the mind's tendency to become entangled in past regrets and future plans, which, if unchecked, can deplete our experience of the present moment. In another form of meditation, people first calm their minds by focusing on the present moment, and then turn their attention to an object of concern and allow themselves to consider the topic from a calm and nonjudgmental frame of awareness. We used both forms of meditation in our Mindful Teacher seminars.

Small-Group Work on Psychological Intrusions

Fifth, after formal sitting meditation, teachers often broke into small groups of dyads or triads to reflect upon topics that intruded upon their consciousness while meditating. On those occasions participants explored the nature of the problem that came to mind and sought new perspectives on it from their colleagues. After a given amount of time—say 20 minutes or half an hour—participants would share their concerns with the group at large.

Through these simple contemplative practices a whole host of topics bloomed forth as generative themes for the group. One teacher resented the manner in which her colleagues so took advantage of her reputation as an effective disciplinarian that, without a single word of warning or explanation, they would send pupils into her classroom whom they couldn't deal with. Another teacher struggled with a colleague who was assigned to her and who on bad days treated the children in her care with thinly veiled contempt. A third teacher was so preoccupied with the misconduct of a child with severe behavioral disorders in her classroom that she hardly could sleep at night in anguish over what the next day would bring.

The purpose of this component of the Mindful Teacher seminars was to examine each of these dilemmas in a situation of calm deliberation and compassionate reflection. In this context we studied Thich Nat Hanh's "Fourteen Mindfulness Trainings" to help us to reflect on the perspectives and experiences of others. The trainings helped us to see the dilemmas for what they actually were—reflections of teachers' having reached their breaking point with students who acted out and the lack of support of the school administration, the pressures of high-stakes testing, or a colleague struggling with her own emotional issues or the the challenges of communicating with an autistic child—and not merely as impediments to raising achievement. The trainings enabled us to inquire into the meanings of these familiar, everyday, but nonetheless intensely experienced dilemmas in all of their breadth and depth to provide mutual support for teachers and colleagues and to explore new possibilities for teaching and learning together. As indicated above, we used a language of "befriending our questions" that arose through meditation and interactions in dyads and triads to create an ambience of open-minded inquiry and reflection.

In this regard it was important for participants to be able to express alternative conceptions and practices in their teaching that contradicted the points of view of the seminar leaders. We had some participants, for example, who were focused on raising pupil achievement with the goal of narrowing the achievement gap between Hispanic and African American students on the one hand and White and Asian pupils on the other. To reach their goals they incorporated a wide variety of practices—choral reading, vocabulary drills, and a regular battery of in-class assessments and curricular adjustments—that in many ways reflected the practices of data-driven decision making that have been criticized earlier in this volume. Yet if the seminar truly was to be a professional setting, and not a site for inculcating a preestablished pedagogical dogma, then it was of the greatest importance that each and every participant engage fully with those practices to explore their strengths and ways that they could be beneficial for the participants' pupils. It is often not so much the practices in and of themselves as it is the ways that they are introduced or implemented in a particular classroom or school context that is beneficial or problematic (Payne, 2008).

The Tuning Protocol

As the group evolved over time, we found that these first 5 stages of the seminar described above—discussions of current developments in the school district, selective vulnerability from a teacher leader, the sharing of scholarly research, mindfulness meditation, and small-group discussion and clarification—often were not enough for the more complex and troubling issues that arose. On such occasions we elected to use a sixth component—the *tuning protocol* developed by activists with the Coalition of Essential Schools—to look more deeply into our concerns (McDonald, Mohr, Dichter, & McDonald, 2007). This protocol allowed us to interrupt the course of a morning's discussions with more extended attention to one particular problem.

How does the tuning protocol work? In the context of a Mindful Teacher seminar, one participant with an especially pressing concern would volunteer to share the issue with the whole group in depth. The participant first would describe the issue while other participants listened silently. Then participants could ask clarifying questions—not questions of interpretation or speculation—for 15 minutes. Then participants would discuss their own interpretations of the situation for a half hour, during which time the presenter could not interrupt or comment. Then the presenter would react with thoughts, with other participants forbidden from speaking. Finally the group would have an open dialogue, followed by a debriefing of the whole activity.

We needed the formal structure of the tuning protocol and the possibilities it opened for rigorous inquiry when dealing with especially troublesome aspects of change that went to the heart of teachers' understandings of their practice. In the first year of the seminar we had two participants who were both science specialists and beginning teachers at the same elementary school. With no malice intended, both teachers were approached by the literacy coach in the building and urged to have the children keep writers' journals in science. And although both teachers were sympathetic to the idea, they bristled at the implication that the content of science as a discipline wasn't just as important as reading and writing.

Yet how can a science teacher—and a beginner at that—respond when one is in an urban school that has to make adequate yearly progress on literacy and math across student subgroups? Should one begin to modify science instruction in order to introduce literacy activities to help the pupils get ready for the state test? Or should one hold fast to the notion that there is a certain disciplinary integrity to science and that, given the short time one has the children each week, exploring the wonders of photosynthesis, electricity, and meteorology really shouldn't be sliced away at to make way for test preparatory activities for another discipline altogether?

Please note: Our Mindful Teacher seminars in many ways were not a venue for *solving* such questions! They *were*, however, a setting for *reflecting* upon the questions with the utmost seriousness of inquiry. Our experience was that such reflection, in and of itself, was experienced by the teachers as *emancipatory*. Contrary to many studies on teaching, we did not find that teachers did not want to theorize their activities. On the contrary. When there is a relentless push for practical solutions, it can be a great relief to understand that in point of fact there often are *only imperfect* pathways forward out of complex dilemmas. Given a supportive collegial setting, teachers in general could see past simplistic oppositions of right and wrong to arrive at more complex judgments about resolutions that would work in some contexts but not in others. And this complex process of decision making and reflection was not viewed as a default option when nothing else worked, but rather as the epitome of the complex and indeterminate art of teaching itself.

In the case presented above, a mindful and selective incorporation of a literacy coach's recommendations, while preserving the core integrity of the discipline of science, was warranted. Here the teachers needed to preserve professional integrity yet be alert to a policy context that could lead to trouble for the school if they were overly principled or rigid. Here the play in the system had to be explored with nuance, skill, and sensitivity to children's own interests and needs. And here respectful engagement with one's colleagues—responding not with anger or pride, but with a questioning approach addressing how teachers as colleagues could best meet children's needs—raised the tone of inquiry to a higher, more intellectual and ethical level of sustainable collegial learning and future professional growth.

Debriefing

The seventh component of the Mindful Teacher seminars involved an *extended debriefing and exploration of opposing themes and experiences.* Here we were especially careful to discourage any and all forms of groupthink that often bedevil not just teachers' work cultures, but those of virtually all professional settings (Campbell, 2005; Lima, 2001). One important manner for signaling respect for the integrity of multiple points of view was that the seminar leaders early on made a point of noting that we ourselves had areas of disagreement and contention with each other about contemporary education. One of us had conducted years of research on community organizing and its potential for improving urban education—but the other had experienced the frustrations of having only three parents out of a class of 20 show up on parents' night. One of us liked the state's MCAS tests because of the way that they held all children to a common standard and provided a focus for instruction—but the other was more critical, worried that excessive attention to the tests was distorting a broad and inclusive curriculum that would allow all children multiple points of entry to learning.

Given the power differences that exist between a university professor and an elementary school teacher, it was important for seminar participants to see that a teacher could feel comfortable challenging a professor to use more down-to-earth language or to be not only abstract but also practical. Likewise, the theoretical challenges that a professor could bring not only to act, but also to think about one's actions, contributed to the group discussions. At times our disagreements with each other became animated arguments, with a vigorous testing out of each other's ideas and our reasons for holding them. Seminar participants joined in during these debates, sometimes favoring interpretations that neither of us held, such as following district mandates from a sense of respect for authority rather than testing them inwardly in light of one's experience and the evidence. Each of us tried to convey to the seminar participants that while we held different points of view, we did not want to make festishes of them, and they should not either. Rather, we viewed them as indispensable points of departure for further learning and growth with each other.

Mindfulness Assignments

The intention, of course, never was to be reflective only in the seminar settings, but rather to practice mindfulness throughout one's personal and professional life. To enhance this goal, the eighth structure of our seminars entailed giving participants tasks that we described as *mindfulness assignments*. Some examples follow:

- We usually are preoccupied with some students in our classrooms and less aware of others. Your assignment is to shift your focus to one or two of the students in your classroom who have been most marginal to your awareness and to write about how that shift in focus changes your relationships with the pupils.
- We have worked in our seminars to "befriend our questions" and to use them as points of departure for sustained inquiry and reflection. Find ways to embed similar practices into your classroom to enable your students to understand the power and validity of their own questions and how they can drive and enrich their learning.
- Examine an area that troubles you in your classroom or school—a new curriculum, a vexed relationship with a colleague, or a stand-off with a pupil that threatens to erode further—and explore ways that you could use mindfulness practices to change how you are viewing the problem and to shift its dynamics.

These assignments then provided bridging activities linking one seminar meeting to the next. They allowed knowledge to accumulate and to become more intricate over time.

WORKING WITH THE TEACHERS' GENERATIVE THEMES: TEN CLUSTERS OF QUESTIONS

Using this eightfold organizational structure, the following 10 *clusters of questions* surfaced in the Mindful Teacher seminars:

- What should I do when my beliefs conflict with new mandates? How should I act when it seems that the district administration is not aware of the on-the-ground realities of my classroom and school?

- How can I preserve my sense of inner dignity and self-respect when I am treated badly by administrators in my building? What possibilities do I have to change the climate in a positive manner by not lashing back reactively but by modeling professional ethics in my own classroom and in my interactions with colleagues?
- How can I bring the demands of my work life under control to preserve a healthy personal life? How can I create some boundaries so that my personal life isn't overwhelmed by my professional obligations?
- Why is there so much inequity within and across schools and school systems? Why are some schools, even within urban systems, awash in resources and support while others struggle just to keep a steady supply of toilet paper and soap in the children's rest rooms?
- What does it mean to be a teacher leader? How can I help to build support networks for teachers in a way that leads to my renewal rather than burnout?
- What do I need to know about to respond effectively to violence in schools and communities? How can my own way of interacting with children, colleagues, and parents in my building contribute to a more peaceful, compassionate environment?
- What adjustments do I need to make to develop the stamina to stay in teaching over the long term? How can we best handle our emotional reactions when we sense that our daily work realities as teachers are not well represented or served?
- How can I help myself to remain mindful of different perspectives and detached from my own point of view, especially when I find myself becoming judgmental or ideological in the press of events? If I accept that the creation of new categories is an important part of mindful learning, how can I stretch my thinking beyond compliance into a new kind of learning that is both more rigorous and creative?
- How can I develop positive relationships with parents and other community members who are important constituencies in my school? How can I contribute to changing historical patterns of mistrust and even animosity to active trust and compassion?
- What factors should we be aware of when we differ from our students in regard to race, class, culture, home language, or gender? What assumptions might we be making or what stereotypes might we hold that have been transmitted to us by the broader culture, and how can we teach against stereotypes in our classrooms while still respecting state standards and curriculum frameworks?

SIX ANCHORING ILLUSTRATIONS

Teachers helped one another to work through these 10 clusters of questions in various ways throughout our seminars. While the teachers' concerns proliferated throughout the seminar, and there were many topics that we could discuss only briefly, *six anchoring illustrations* will now be presented to provide examples of the kinds of cases teachers brought to seminar discussions. Each of the cases is related to one or more of the clusters of questions above, and shows how mindful teaching, while not an elixir for problems that have historical and institutional features that go far beyond a given teacher's capacities to resolve, can provide a valuable point of departure for understanding and addressing the problems.

OLIVIA JONES: TEACHING THE CIVIL RIGHTS MOVEMENT IN THE AGE OF ACCOUNTABILITY

Olivia Jones[1] knew from a very early age that she wanted to be a teacher. Her parents brought her up in a loving, religious environment that left her with a strong social responsibility to learn about and care for others. She attended an urban public school system in New York State in which she experienced a very positive diverse environment, and decided that she wanted to work in a similar secondary school. She started teaching right after college at an urban school and soon, in 2003, entered a masters degree program at Boston College geared for urban teachers. After completing the program she was hired at Clark, a middle school in Boston.

Olivia shudders when she remembers her early teaching experiences, which she describes as "insane! When I went to Clark, it was almost as if I had never taught before. We were constantly breaking up fights and the teachers were always being ridiculed by the principal. My kids have nothing. My school is like a dumping ground. We have some parents who try their hardest, and are willing to help, and we have others hang up on us when we call them."

She was also stunned by how the administration and the faculty were divided. "We were not unified. Our principal was a dictator, and teachers shut down pretty quickly. It was so crazy that first year. Only at the end of it did some of the teachers begin calling each other by our first names." Slowly a small group of teachers began cohering and helping one another.

Olivia knew from her own experiences and from research on urban education that it is extremely important to have a schoolwide culture that holds the children to high standards. Under the leadership of Superintendent Tom Payzant, the BPS already had endorsed a model of "Whole School Improvement Plans" to help create such cultures. In her own building, however, there really was no common culture shared among the faculty; the teachers were utterly "balkanized" (Hargreaves, 1994, p. 213). The only thing they shared in common was their fear of the principal and the trust of a small group of colleagues, usually based in the same team and working with the same children.

One of Olivia 's major crises as a teacher occurred when she planned a large interdisciplinary unit on the history of the civil rights movement, with guest speakers, films, and a wide variety of readings. She found that her students were galvanized by the readings and she hoped to inspire and impress her principal by inviting him into the classroom to see what her pupils had accomplished. She was shocked when the principal appeared apathetic in regard to the unit and instead insisted on making sure that she was teaching the students to pass the MCAS.

In many ways, the Mindful Teacher seminars were designed to reach out to and support struggling urban teachers like Olivia. When she first joined the seminar, accumulated wounds of years of intimidation and isolation had taken a toll. She provided harrowing descriptions of verbal abuse that teachers endured at the hands of her principal. She needed a safe environment in which she could describe how bizarre it was to have her principal do a teaching evaluation of her when he couldn't even spell her last name properly and virtually never was seen in her part of the building except when a crisis occurred or when he was conducting teacher evaluations.

Just as it was important for Olivia to describe the climate of fear and oppression in which she worked every day, it was also important for us as seminar leaders to return to the concepts of mindfulness that provided the conceptual undergirding of our seminar. What processes occur that lead idealistic educators, who enter the profession with all kinds of exalted hopes, to become worn down with the passage of time and to end up as authoritarian administrators who view their colleagues as enemies rather than as allies? Do teachers understand and appreciate the anxieties of parents and the public in general over whether their children are achieving academically, and do they appreciate the contributions, and not just harp on the flaws, of accountability systems that in point of fact are designed to improve pupil learning? What resources do teachers have to persuade administrators and the public that they really do have children's best interests at heart, and that they endorse the goals of high levels of academic achievement that virtually all Americans wish for our young people?

The Mindful Teacher seminar supported Olivia not just by validating her integrity as a professional and a human being, but also by moving her through our eightfold structure in a way that enabled her to break out of her defensive formations to acknowledge the complexity of the social situation in which she was working. By starting with an examination of the vulnerabilities of teachers, she could see that she was not alone and that her own private problems as an educator had a social dimension that was in many ways beyond her control. By looking deeply into the multiple pressures placed upon her principal, she could come to understand his exasperation and challenges in trying to keep his building from spinning out of control. A brief excursus on the intersection of race, poverty, and social control in urban schools could help to remind us that the problems of urban education did not originate with this principal and that American society has failed at providing an equitable education to our most disadvantaged children.

Shortly after discussing Olivia's situation we invited in two former upper-level administrative leaders from the BPS to speak with us at the Mindful Teacher seminar. The administrators explained their own challenges in attempting to provide adequate support and oversight of the 150 schools in the district—a task easier said than done when one considers the continual emergence of crises that demand immediate attention and subvert the kind of careful, long-term planning needed to create systemic change. They expressed their frustrations with union guidelines that make the removal of poor teachers so long and onerous that administrators generally decide to put up with the worst teachers rather than remove them. They also reminded the teachers that many of the reforms that had been piloted by the Boston Public Schools—the funding of literacy, math, and curriculum coaches, for example, or the institutionalization of "collaborative coaching and learning"—were designed not to oppress teachers but to provide them with additional resources for reflecting upon and improving their teaching (Reville, 2007). From their side of the table, so to speak, they experienced in a negative form what Linda Darling-Hammond (1990) has described as "the power of the base over the top" (p. 339), discovering that some teachers rejected out of hand even the most rigorous of new research findings in favor of traditional practices that had failed with students in the past and most likely would continue doing so in the future.

After hearing from the two former administrators and learning of their own frustrations at simply not having enough time to improve learning in a vast network of very different schools in very different communities, the teachers in the seminar began to soften their criticisms of administrators. They came to appreciate that administrators, too, were exasperated at working in an underfunded school system with many bureaucratic guidelines in place that were a disservice to pupils. The duality of "us against them" began to be replaced by a more complex understanding of a whole range of forces that lead to depersonalization and dehumanization, with no obvious single force or factor available to play the role of villain.

The contribution of the Mindful Teacher seminars in this instance was not a direct intervention that raises test scores, but rather the creation of a more multifaceted approach to the social dynamics of an urban school, allowing a more empathic, open-minded spirit of inquiry and problem solving to emerge. The seminars cannot, of course, stop an administrator from abusing teachers—but they *can* provide teachers with a new frame for understanding their administrators, for discussing skillful and unskillful ways of working with them, and for discovering common ground. An in-depth study of the Civil Rights Movement should not be diluted or distorted to become just another topic for test preparation, but the opposition between subject knowledge depth and test preparation may be more fluid and negotiable than sometimes appears the case. The English language sections of the state test, for example, ask students to demonstrate their abilities to read texts closely, to discern multiple points of view, and to advance an independent and original line of interpretation. One can use all of these skills to debate Martin Luther King, Jr.'s decision to use children to protest segregated facilities during the Birmingham campaign in 1963, for example—a strategy denounced by Malcolm X but one that decisively shifted public opinion in favor of the Civil Rights Movement. But teachers and administrators are unlikely to discover such common ground unless they have some assistance in doing so—especially in light of the pressures placed upon educators to respond reactively in a climate of high-stakes accountability systems.

Olivia's experiences demonstrate the importance of guided assistance when negative experiences lead teachers to resort to patterns of defensiveness that obscure ongoing inquiry and the search for new categories of meaning-making that can overcome apparent oppositions. In many ways, her experiences illuminate the salience of Ellen Langer's understanding of mindfulness as openness to new experience and the engendering of new categories of understanding. With such greater mindfulness, the paralyzing "Ingroup Virtue/Outgroup Vice" polarity that Charles Payne (2008, p. 26) has documented among urban teachers can begin to be addressed as a major impediment to raising social trust and social capital in the urban school environment. Needless to say, such open-mindedness and introspection among teachers can be successful only if they are matched by similar attributes among administrators.

MEGAN MAHONEY:
FROM MEDITATION TO CLASSROOM QUIET TIME

Mindfulness in another form, quiet attentiveness, with greater similarities to traditional Buddhist practices, can be found in the experiences of Megan Mahoney, a special educator in the BPS. Megan found the practice of meditation in the Mindful Teacher seminars to be an especially calming balm after a week of stressful instruction. In her journal, she described the value of meditation for her as follows:

> When I first joined the Mindful Teacher project 4 years ago, I had no idea what to expect. I knew that I would be meeting with other teachers who were placed in urban settings to share and reflect upon our experiences. One tool that we began to explore was meditation and the 14 different "mindfulness trainings" of Thich Nhat Hanh. As we began, I have to admit that I was quite skeptical of meditation. But when we meditated at each of our meetings, I found myself beginning to look forward to and appreciating the time that was set aside for meditation at each of our Mindful Teacher meetings. I truly enjoyed that time to myself. I felt free to think freely and uninterrupted and could truly begin to reflect on my students, my classroom, my teaching, and my own personal life. As a teacher, there is so little time set aside to quiet your mind. At times I was able to really clear my head, or to wrap my mind around a different issue in my classroom at this time.

In the first seminars we began simply by practicing calming meditation together, and we then added concentration meditations. Participants first would calm their minds, and we then would ask them to turn their attention to their classrooms to observe those topics that were preoccupying them. In Megan's case, after an early meditation session together, she shared that she was preoccupied with two boys in her class who were especially demanding of her time. "The more I worked with one who had special behavior issues," she commented, "the worse he became. I went so far as to keep him after school to give him individual help. It didn't make the changes I thought it would." Several other teachers chimed in, sharing that they felt especially guilty toward well-behaved students who received far less attention than those who were acting out and disrupting instruction.

As a special educator working in a substantially separate environment with a small group of students identified with a range of learning disabilities, Megan experienced high levels of frustration daily. She had learned in her teacher education program that she needed to be acutely aware of the alternative needs of children with learning disabilities that so often are coupled with social and emotional challenges. In identifying those needs, Megan knew it was her responsibility to personalize instruction for the pupils by capitalizing on their previous knowledge bases and skills.

Yet Megan also knew that special educators had fought long and hard to ensure that children with special needs would no longer be exempted from state examinations. Advocacy groups argued that the on-the-ground reality of schools simply was that unless children were tested, they were not going to receive any concentrated attention. This lack of attention itself became such a major social justice issue that groups such as the National Council for Learning Disabilities lobbied Congress so that the No Child Left Behind Act would mandate that all children with special needs be assessed just like everyone else. Consequently, Megan found that she needed to norm her instruction so that her students—who represented the school's subcategory of special needs—would achieve proficiency on the MCAS tests, thereby securing adequate yearly progress.

These policy changes had direct ramifications for Megan's classroom. When she first began teaching, the majority of her time with her pupils was spent on remediation. Her students had to take MCAS examinations, but because there was no high-stakes accountability in regard to the results, they received insufficient attention either within the school or the district. As a result of the recent reforms, however, it now was incumbent upon Megan to keep up with the grade-level pacing guides, which include ongoing assessments of pupil progress.

Megan found classroom management to be the most challenging during the assessment periods. Students would break down and cry or storm out of the classroom. Megan tried to reassure the students that they could indeed do the test, but inside her heart was breaking because she knew just how humiliating it was for the children to have their inabilities exposed to them with such little sensitivity to their special needs.

It was during one of these critical incidents that, with the teachers in the seminar, we developed our own home-spun "mindfulness interventions" in the spirit of Ellen Langer. We decided that we would try to direct our attention to a student in our class who was most on the periphery of our awareness and away from the student(s) who demanded disproportionate amounts of attention from us. When Megan began trying to regulate her behavior in this manner, she immediately found that it was challenging in respect to one of her boys: "It is difficult to ignore attention-seeking behaviors from across the room," she wrote in her journal. "The key seems to be keeping the other students from getting involved in his behavior." Yet she was willing slowly to shift her attention in a deliberate manner to the other students who were trying to learn. Although it took time and careful scaffolding, the problematic student ultimately benefited by becoming more self-regulating. At the end of this small intervention, Megan wrote, "Hopefully this withdrawal of constant attention over time will increase his chances of success in the following years."

Megan was especially concerned that her students who acted out most were having a negative impact on other students, both by distracting her and by indicating that disrespect and impulsivity were prime ways to gain the teacher's attention. Her solution to the problem was both to increase the attention that she gave to quieter students and to build "quiet time" into the day when students could "reflect about the day or about issues the kids were having." She wanted the students to think not only about classroom activities, but also about their own thinking and to observe how it changed during the course of a day. "Lately, after a big outing or test or sometimes when the students look stressed, we stop and have 10 minutes of quiet reflection time," she reported.

Although teaching is never easy and predictable, Megan found that by redirecting her attention, and by building an atmosphere in her classroom that created a more calm and attentive environment, her class became more manageable and focused. Intriguingly, it was *not* a matter of doing more in the sense of preparing more and better activities. Nor was it a matter of aligning her instruction with tests, or using data to drive her decision making, or any of the other reforms that are most discussed in policy circles today. Rather, the simple opening into a calm time that enabled students to process the events of the day and to be more attuned to what was going on inside and outside of themselves seemed to make the difference. "As this past month has progressed, it is clear that by consciously shifting my attention from the one student who consumed my thoughts both in and out of school, I was able to create a shift in my classroom community dynamic," she wrote. "That quiet time meant more to the students than talk time with me."

RENEE SIMMONS: SAFETY AS A PRECONDITION FOR LEARNING

Renee Simmons had a child when she was in her third year of undergraduate studies at Northeastern University. She was preparing to be an elementary school teacher with a minor in special education. However, after the birth of her son she realized that she was not going to be able to continue with her studies and dropped out to get a full-time job at a local YMCA. When her son turned 4 and entered the BPS, she was still working full-time and struggling to make ends meet. Eventually, with the support of community members, including those from her church, Renee was able to complete her degree in education and in 2003 she obtained a position with the Boston Public Schools.

Renee began as a kindergarten teacher in her 1st year, was switched to fifth grade in her 2nd year (because of her low level of seniority), and became a first-grade teacher in her 3rd year. The switching was hectic but necessary because of declining enrollments in the neighborhood where she worked. What concerned Renee more than the overwhelming demands of switching grades, learning new curriculum, and designing new lessons, however, was the disconnect between the school in which she worked and the communities from which the children came.

From Renee's perspective, she sees a school district in which the vast majority of teachers are unfamiliar with (and too many lack curiosity about) the community conditions BPS pupils have experienced. Because she lives in the same section of the city as many BPS students, she herself knows firsthand how unsettling it is to wake up after a restless night, when police helicopters circle overhead with their search lights on, potentially helping with crime protection, but also awakening sleeping children and contributing to an atmosphere of round-the-clock anxiety and surveillance. And she knows not only tragedy when young people are attacked and even killed as gang violence spins out of control, but also the broader impact when children are afraid to play outside, and even riding a crowded city bus in the middle of an afternoon is no shelter from senseless shootings and robberies.

In the spring of 2007, teachers at Renee's school began hearing story after story from their pupils about incidents of bullying and fights on the school bus. Because of Boston's choice model, children can travel all the way across the city, making for a bus ride of close to an hour for some of her pupils. By listening to the children, Renee gradually was able to piece together the many mosaic stones of a problem that was undermining learning for far too many children.

Bored on the buses, and with no adult supervision other than that provided by the driver, older pupils began taunting younger ones to fight one another, with regular altercations and many tears shed even before the children arrived at school in the morning. Teachers began hearing about parents who had threatened to kill students who had begun fights with their children on the school buses, and police began reporting more and more incidents of students throwing things out of windows or causing serious injuries to one another as playful jostling turned into serious physical attacks. Problems like these had been occurring for years, but the situation seemed utterly out of control that spring.

During our Mindful Teacher seminar meetings, we discussed the division between the schools and the communities that had been a gaping wound in Boston for decades. The infamous school busing crises of the

1970s only exposed a decades-old pattern of racism and social exclusion that led parents of color to suspect the motives of teachers and administrators in the school system. In our seminar setting, we asked ourselves how the teachers in Renee's school could best respond to the situation. We learned that the district was planning to respond by dividing the pupils on one of the most troubled buses into two separate buses. Despite this potential remedy, problems persisted to the point where one student in particular pleaded with Renee for protection.

Aware that young children really can't concentrate on learning when they are fearful of imminent physical attacks, Renee made an independent decision that she no longer could tolerate the situation, and, as a result, she began riding the school bus with the children from her home in Roxbury to her school each day. Renee's presence on the bus immediately changed the atmosphere of anxiety and tension experienced by the children. Because she was known as a strict disciplinarian who also was devoted to the children's well-being, the fighting among the children entirely stopped. The children were able to arrive at school calm, concentrated, and able to begin the day focused on learning.

Unlike Renee, most urban educators do not come from urban environments themselves. Their own backgrounds are suburban or rural, and their racial identity is White, not African American. Hence, their point of departure for approaching the urban setting is a fundamentally different one, based on different life experiences and identities. In the Mindful Teacher seminars, Renee had a venue for discussing her own deeply rooted commitment to advancing social justice as an urban educator and the challenges of living in a community with many needs that urban public schools often address imperfectly.

Renee's experiences provided a springboard for the Mindful Teacher seminars to delve into scholarship on community organizing, the achievement gap, and multicultural education. Why is it that so many Black boys struggle in school, and why does the achievement gap widen rather than narrow as young people progress through school? Why is it that decades after the Civil Rights Movement so few teachers of color are in so many urban schools today? How can teachers engage their students in discussions of race and class when many of their schools leave these themes unspoken, in spite of their students' craving for meaningful and open discourse?

By asking these questions, seminar participants were searching for ways to understand some of the most complex and challenging social justice issues in American society today. Teachers fear that they will be blamed for the achievement gap without any consideration of out-of-school influences on learning, and parents in communities of color, rightly observing that their children receive less per-pupil funding and in the aggregate, are taught by less qualified teachers than children in suburban districts, respond by doubting the ability and commitment of educators to their children. Race is deeply implicated in these matters and so is class.

These fault lines between predominantly White teaching forces and urban communities of color first came to a head in major battles in northern cities like New York and Boston in the 1960s and 1970s, and their legacies still persist decades later (Formisano, 1991; Perlstein, 2004). To develop an alternative vision of how educators and parents have overcome their mistrust of one another and collaborated, seminar participants read case studies of community organizing for school reform (Shirley, 1997, 2002, 2007). While the case studies could not provide anything close to a final solution to these complex problems, they did provide numerous organizing strategies that teachers could develop to transform schools from outposts of a bureaucracy to centers of pupil achievement and civic engagement.

JEFF TIMBERLAKE:
FROM THE NOBEL PEACE PRIZE TO MCAS CAMP

It's one thing when devoted educators like Renee volunteer to expand their roles to deal with a critical impasse in a school's culture, but it's another altogether when administrators make it their job to make incursions into teachers' private time to impose additional test-preparatory activities. To understand how jarring the difference can be between *initiating* independent action and instead feeling like one is on the *receiving end* of others' expectations, it is helpful to turn to the case of a beginning teacher who found himself struggling to stay in the urban environment at the end of his first year.

Jeff Timberlake was a career changer who entered a teacher education program in 2005 that required him to teach for a full year as a student teacher in the Boston Public Schools. He was assigned to a second-grade teacher who gave him enormous encouragement and support to explore his own ideas and to develop his own signature practices. A high point came for him when he had the opportunity to develop a thematic unit of study on a topic of his own choosing. He consulted the state standards for guidance and then set about creating an interdisciplinary set of lessons about Africa that he hoped would address the social studies standard on leadership.

In the course of his research, Jeff learned about the inspiring political leadership of Dr. Wangari Maathai, a Kenyan human rights activist and environmentalist who launched the "Greenbelt Movement" in Africa that has led to planting over 40 million trees to prevent soil erosion (Maathai, 2004). A truly courageous and independent thinker, Maathai was imprisoned and violently attacked on multiple occasions for protesting political corruption in her native land. She founded the Mazingira Green Party of Kenya in 2003, became the first African woman to receive the Nobel Peace Prize in 2004, and was chosen to lead the United Nation's "One Billion Trees Campaign" in 2006.

Jeff originally thought that it would be wonderful if his students could plant trees on school property and thus make their own contribution to Dr. Maathai's campaign for sustainable development, but his school had little soil available for planting except for two small flower beds. Instead, he decided to involve students in an art activity of creating their own trees while using readings on Dr. Maathai to teach students about African geography, history, and culture.

Shortly after Jeff had introduced the leadership unit, Dr. Maathai was chosen to be one of eight flag bearers at the 2006 winter Olympics. One of his students was watching the Olympics with his parents, recognized Dr. Maathai, and was able to describe her leadership to his family. Jeff then wrote a letter to Dr. Maathai, explained to her that he was using her in a unit of study, and informed her that the students were really interested in her work for sustainable development. She wrote back and he read the letter to the students. "They were pretty blown away by that!" he recalled. "The children felt like they were learning something that wasn't common knowledge to everyone."

At the end of his first year, Jeff received a teaching position at a school that previously had been struggling to meet adequate yearly progress and had received a warning in accordance with NCLB policy guidelines. Rallying all of its forces and concentrating on raising achievement, the school subsequently registered test score gains and then was awarded a substantial amount of supplementary funding. Jeff approached the position with enthusiasm and knew that the school administrators were eager to continue with the school's new upward trajectory.

Jeff was disturbed, however, to discover that numerous concessions had to be made as part of this drive to support achievement. Outdoor recess had been curtailed in the school, limiting the amount of time his third graders had for exercise and to gain valuable social skills with less adult supervision. Jeff enjoyed the fact that students ate breakfast in their teachers' classrooms but found it frustrating that morning mealtime needed to be accompanied by morning math work. Jeff commented:

> When I first got to the school, I was told by other teachers that
> due to the most recent MCAS scores, the level of stress was

up among the administration, and that in turn was felt by the teachers working there. It was immediately made clear to me that I would not have a lot of autonomy in my classroom. Walk-throughs were done to ensure I was following the schedule and that my content and language objectives were written on the whiteboard. At the time, my feeling was that involving my students with a unit on leadership would not have been supported. The school climate appeared intense. In hindsight, I think some of that intensity was a direct result of the input that I was getting from my peers. There's a process of learning to distance yourself from the chatter going on around you. Still, I remember feeling overwhelmed by the schedule that had been given to me and believed that straying away from it might lead to an unsatisfactory comment in my end-of-the-year teacher evaluation. The majority of my teaching day was devoted to math. I had little, if any, time for one-on-one conferences with my students. I knew this was disadvantageous to my students' growth, but didn't know how to fit those reading and writing conferences into a schedule that was encumbered by the required 90 minutes of math a day.

As the year progressed, Jeff took on additional responsibilities such as teaching after-school sessions 4 days a week and teaching MCAS camp on Saturdays. As a first-year teacher, he found himself drowning in the new high-stakes environment of testing and accountability, with precious little restorative time to reflect on his own learning or to customize his instruction and curriculum to the children in his class. Jeff originally had entered teaching because he was eager to ignite a love of lifelong learning in young children, but he soon found himself suffocating in the environment of his school. Jeff recalls, "It was an emotionally and physically taxing year for me. I had serious questions about my effectiveness as a teacher in urban education. Ironically, I had to take on another commitment—the Mindful Teacher seminar—to allow myself the permission to reflect upon those questions of effectiveness which kept me up at night."

When we shared the Mindful Teacher intervention about focusing on one child who had been on the periphery of participants' awareness, Jeff leaped on the opportunity to dedicate himself to Gregorio, a Salvadoran boy who was always attentive but rarely assertive. He decided to make a book for Gregorio about El Salvador that included a colorful map showing the different provinces, a picture of the country's flag, action pictures of the national soccer team, and some information about El Salvador's Bosque El Imposible National Park.

The following day, during Jeff's scheduled guided reading block, he decided to engage in dialogue with Gregorio about the book. "As a result of trying to meet the demands of my schedule every day, I had inadvertently shifted the focus of my teaching away from the identities of my students and toward checking off things on my list. As I approached this conversation with Gregorio, I felt a certain amount of fear and anxiety melting away." Jeff discovered that Gregorio not only loved soccer but also played the sport with a children's team after school. "After that live encounter with my student, I truly felt reenergized to teach. What's more, Gregorio returned to class the next day with a new energy to learn!"

Jeff is not fluent in Spanish, but he is able to engage in simple conversations with dominant-Spanish speakers. He remembers a change in Gregorio's mother's demeanor when she dropped off Gregorio at the school in the morning. "She smiled at me," Jeff remembers. Jeff felt proud of the plurality in his classroom—there were students representing languages and customs from several countries—and pleased that he was finding his way back to the idealism that had expressed itself in his project on Dr. Mathaai.

Jeff continues to teach because he believes he is good at what he does, and although it is difficult, he is finding that he possesses the inner resources and external supports to create an exciting and engaging classroom environment while maintaining mindful awareness of the broader school and social contexts. "Honestly, when I find myself overwhelmed by the day or ineffective in my ability to meet the daily pacing guide, I just stop and breathe," he comments. "I remember the importance of my live encounter with that student during my first year of teaching and I then find new ways to stay connected with the children I have in my classroom now."

GRACE NAPOLITANO AND MAGGIE SLYE:
MINDFUL DATA ANALYSIS

At the outset of this volume, we criticized the current popularity of data-driven decision making for reducing the complex intellectual process of teaching to simplistic overreactions to limited and in many ways arbitrary assessment measures, particularly annually administered high-stakes tests. Jeff's case indicates the distortions that can occur when testing takes precedence over a loving and caring attitude toward children. But our criticism of DDDM is misunderstood if one infers that we are opposed to all forms of data gathering and use. Teachers, like any other professionals, need to study and use data to inform their decisions. Just like doctors, lawyers, or engineers, teachers need to track the impact of their decisions and to make modifications of their judgments, while staying alert to data sets that do not triangulate with one another or test score gains that are spurious because they are not generalizable.

Two teachers in the Mindful Teacher project exemplify how teachers can use data to refine their reflective judgment and to engage others in the process of collaborative learning. When Grace Napolitano first came to the project in her third year of urban teaching, she was exhausted by an unusually demanding inclusion classroom. For Grace the seminars were a lifeline to a world of other professionals who recognized the daunting challenges of teaching today and were eager to develop their skills to teach to the very best of their ability. She described the simple emotional support that the seminar offered as a form of "therapy" that helped her to understand that her difficulties with behavioral management were not of her own making, but had to do with the manner in which her classroom was "stacked" with those fourth-grade pupils whose learning and behavioral needs were the greatest in her school.

Grace survived the year, after many sleepless nights wracked with anxiety about what the next day might bring, but not without wondering whether she had erred in entering teaching. But behind the emotional toll, she was left wondering how she could respond quickly and effectively to classroom environments or even individual pupils that seemed to spin out of control at the smallest disturbance. She knew that simply complaining about a stacked classroom, or even pointing out the dubious legality of such pupil assignments in light of federal laws mandating mainstreaming and the provision of least restrictive environments, was likely to garner little sympathy or support from overworked administrators in an understaffed school. For Grace, the solution came through accepting and capitalizing upon the emphasis on careful documentation and data gathering that has been so prominent in recent reforms.

In the fall of 2008, Grace found herself struggling to teach Miguel, a student who was especially disruptive, whether through singing, humming, lack of body control, or laughing uncontrollably at inappropriate times, such as when a classmate was sharing an idea or reading aloud. Grace thought that Miguel might have attention deficit hyperactivity disorder and contacted Miguel's mother, who set up an appointment with Miguel's doctor to have him assessed. Yet because she knew that urban pupils tend to be referred disproportionately for special education services, she was reluctant to pursue this route if she could discover a way of helping Miguel. But in the interim, what could she do to establish a sense of order and focused attention to learning in her classroom?

Grace worked with her student teacher from Boston College, Marlene Gomez, to study and then to modify Miguel's behavior. In her journal, Grace wrote that the first step of this applied behavioral analysis was simple documentation, so "we broke the day up by subject, then further segmenting each subject into 5-minute increments. This would be our 'data-keeping' sheet. We then took data for 7 days." If Miguel disrupted the class, "we would put a check mark. Sometimes, we would address the behavior, other times we would ignore it depending on how intrusive it was to the class."

What did the data-keeping sheet reveal? Grace "calculated that Miguel missed 930 minutes, or 15.5 hours, of instructional time over that 7-day period. We looked at where we saw the most checks, and we found that literacy (reading, writing, and phonics) is where we found the highest rate of checks." Grace then worked with Miguel to identify rewards that he would like to earn and were realistic as a result of modifying his behavior. His rewards included stickers on a chart, a stroll with Grace or Marlene around the school, or choice time at the end of the school day when he could play on the computer, do a puzzle, or play a board game with a friend.

Miguel did not respond immediately to the new incentive system, but after about 2 weeks, his behavior began improving. "He was now able to sit without interrupting the group," Grace wrote. "As a result, Miguel was able to complete his work more efficiently because he had attended to the lessons and understood the objective and material that was being presented." While Miguel's disruptions continued, they decreased "dramatically, to on average five interruptions per day. This was a significant change in behavior. As a result of this information, we decided that Miguel was not in need of additional services. It appears that Miguel just needs positive attention in a more structured way."

Grace helped Miguel to develop the social skills and self-control to show proper respect for his classmates, his teacher, and his own learning. Concomitantly, Grace's intervention with Miguel was successful in terms of tracking his literacy gains. In the period from September 2008 to January 2009, Miguel's Developmental Reading Assessment results moved from "pre-emergent" to "emergent," thereby showing progress.

Maggie Slye, another seminar participant, shows a different dimension of mindful data analysis. Like Grace, Maggie has developed her skills in documenting pupil behavior and learning. In terms of literacy instruction, Maggie's perspective is that the data that she has gathered through miscue analyses have revealed that her struggling readers "relied almost entirely on meaning cues, and were stymied by long vowels, digraphs, consonant blends, and diphthongs." Based on this information, Maggie looked for and learned about "a word study program that was explicit, systematic, and included components I felt were essential to lock in letters–sound knowledge, such as decodable text and kinesthetics." After adding the program to her literacy block, she was delighted to discover that "most of my students' reading levels improved by 1.5 years" in the space of a single academic year. "While there could be countless explanations for their growth, I believe the data I collected during my miscue analyses, and the instructional decisions I made based on those data, substantially contributed to their success."

Maggie eagerly studies a variety of data as measures of pupil learning and believes it is her responsibility to confer individually with her pupils to explain their test results and to provide the support and confidence that will motivate them to excel on the tests. This understanding of the value of data is connected with her strong ethic of social justice and democratic transparency. Professional expertise, in this perspective, makes it incumbent on all educators continually to learn about their pupils' learning and to engage pupils themselves in reflecting on how they best learn. Urban teachers have a special obligation to be committed to social justice, Maggie argues, and social justice cannot be achieved if educators themselves do not have crucial information about their students' lives both in and out of school. In one of her writings, Maggie explained:

> I think that another important aspect of being a mindful teacher is being aware of the important influences in our students' lives. We collect data on our students' interests to better match them to books that they will love. This, in turn, nurtures a love of reading. We collect data on our students' cultures and traditions to better recognize and honor our students' individual experiences. This, in turn, fosters a safe, welcoming, and respectful classroom environment that is optimal for learning. Part of collecting data about our students so that we know how to better serve them, is creating strong, respectful relationships with their families.

Both Grace and Maggie show that learning to document and study student behavior is an important part of what we are describing here as "mindful data analysis." In the examples above, each teacher took the initiative to identify breakdowns in teaching and learning and to modify her own reactions to the problems to promote pupil learning. In each example, the teacher was a creative problem solver and independent thinker who demonstrated the fortitude to go beyond simple identification of a problem to refine her analyses through careful empirical study and consequent pedagogical change.

Each teacher, however, was cautious to note that it takes considerable amounts of time to design instruments, gather data, and then design and measure the impacts of new interventions. One teacher who had studied

data-driven decision making in one of our classes at Boston College com-
·mented dryly, "I went into teaching because I loved working with kids,
but I guess it's time to forget all of that and just get a lab coat!" Behind
the irreverence and hyperbole of her comment stands an important insight: Teachers can't do everything. Data analysis, if it is to be done well,
requires a tremendous amount of time. As Maggie commented:

> If we want our teachers to be mindful, and to make decisions
> based on what they know, not just what they feel, we have to
> give teachers the instructional flexibility and time to respond to
> the data. This is not to say that being mindful means never fol-
> lowing a pacing guide, but teachers must be given the time during
> the school day to also address the gaps in understanding the data
> may present. For leaders to say they value data-driven instruc-
> tion, but then not allow their teachers to adjust their instruction
> or schedule based on data, is a mixed message.

KARYN CIRULLI:
SUPPORTIVE CHANGES FOR TEACHERS AND CHILDREN

Karyn Cirulli came to Boston from a suburban town in Pennsylvania,
where she had completed an undergraduate program geared toward urban education. Many of her relatives, whom she had always looked up
to as a child, had been teachers, and she always knew that she wanted to
be a teacher, too.

When Karyn first attempted to apply for a job in the BPS, she was
discouraged by what she experienced as an unbelievably onerous and dis-
organized process. The BPS human resources employees were unfriendly,
and when she arrived for an interview at an agreed-upon time at one
middle school, the principal was nowhere to be found. Karyn was re-
lieved and excited when she finally was called and offered a position as a
first-grade teacher.

Karyn views the major challenge of education today to be the lack of
support provided to an overwhelmingly needy population of students.
She teaches in an underperforming school that has been designated a
"superintendent's school" to receive additional assistance—little of which
actually has been forthcoming. In addition to their academic needs, the
students require lots of emotional attention. Many of her pupils struggle
with issues of abandonment, have witnessed abusive relationships, and
live in violent neighborhoods where drug dealing and random shootings

have become common. There is only one school counselor in the building of over 400 children. Their emotional needs are rarely met at school, and policy makers' press for academic achievement has played a role in diminishing reflection about those needs.

Karyn has found that she has not been able to teach as she would like because behavioral problems impede her efficacy as an instructor. One year she had an especially difficult situation with a girl named Cecilia in her class whose father had abandoned her and whose mother was in jail. Cecilia was being raised by an aunt, but the Department of Social Services became involved when it appeared that the apartment where she lived was unsafe and her aunt may have disciplined her in abusive ways. Without a moment's notice, Cecilia would leave Karyn's first-grade classroom in the midst of instruction. The protocol in the school was for teachers to contact the principal's office when a child left the classroom, but when Karyn did so, no one was there to help. The secretary often was gone from the office, as was the principal. So sometimes Karyn chased after Cecilia, leaving her classroom unsupervised, and at other times she simply decided she could not leave the children in her classroom, thereby allowing Cecilia to wander alone throughout the building. But each and every time that the running occurred, she found herself psychologically split in two, worried about Cecilia and distracted while trying to teach all of the other children who were in the class and deserving of her instruction.

When she shared her difficulties with a teacher from across the hallway, she learned that that the other teacher also had students with behavioral issues who required constant attention and she could not help Karyn. In subsequent years, Karyn was hopeful when she learned that her school would receive a specialist in behavioral management. In point of fact, however, the new resident expert seemed to know little about how to communicate with children. Instead, he himself would let them run in the halls when he decided that he had no idea of what to do with them.

When Karyn shared this situation with the other Mindful Teacher seminar participants, she inadvertently unleashed a torrent of similar stories from teachers who felt that they were utterly on their own even when in a building with hundreds of children and dozens of teachers. Teachers shared their own experiences of dealing with rebellious and violent children with no one else to assist, of altercations with parents, and of children with special needs placed inappropriately in their classrooms without legally required supports in place. Karyn's story was about a child in trouble, but it was also about a teacher who did not know how to respond swiftly and appropriately—and who also knew that she was legally liable for the safety of each child placed in her care.

Karyn's response to this situation was to set up a "quiet table" where children could be in a safe and semiprivate place when there was too much stimulation in the class and they needed their own area. She was delighted when Cecilia responded positively to the table and would use it to write what she was feeling inside. Karyn found that Cecilia wrote about how she missed her mother and how she wished that she could talk with her and go shopping with her and do all of the normal kinds of activities that girls love to do with their mothers. Karyn's heart went out to her, and she tried to encourage Cecilia that one day things would get better, although she herself didn't know what the future really would hold for her.

Karyn's creative response of setting up a special writing area for Cecilia did not stop her incidences of leaving the classroom without a moment's notice. But Karyn did notice a real change, because Cecilia began coming back to the classroom of her own accord and then heading straight to the quiet table, where she would write what she was feeling. Cecilia was beginning to find her own way of dealing with her emotions and impulsiveness, and while Karyn still didn't like it that she would leave the classroom, she came to expect that Cecilia would return on her own—and her expectations were fulfilled.

Karyn's case illustrates some of the real pain and uncertainty that can accompany mindful teaching. Teachers often are in situations where no one can really help them. Administrators are too busy or are unavailable; their fellow teachers have their own classes and can't leave them when a crisis occurs; parents and paraprofessionals are in and out of buildings and can't be relied upon to be magically available when the unexpected occurs. Instead, teachers have to fall back on their own intuition and best guesses of ways to respond to children. This loneliness of teaching carries enormous emotional costs for teachers. For Karyn, it was especially hard to hold out hope for Cecilia—she herself had always had a very close relationship with her own mother and could hardly begin to imagine how much it must hurt to have one's mother in jail—but she knew that it was her personal and professional responsibility to keep hoping in spite of the odds. Truly, one has no choice to stop hoping—for without that, one becomes part of a problem rather than a solution in children's lives.

LEARNING FROM THE SIX ILLUSTRATIONS

What do we learn from our six anchoring illustrations of what we are calling mindful teaching? If you are a classroom teacher, we anticipate that as you read through the cases, you found many ways that you could identify with each of the teachers. While we hope that you never have experienced verbal abuse from an administrator as Olivia did, chances are high that you have experienced conflict with administrators and have wondered how you can best advance children's interests in the light of pressing policy demands. Both Megan and Karyn were struggling with ways to shape their classrooms into peaceful and safe environments where pupils could first feel secure and then focus on their learning—certainly a universal concern for educators. Renee's unusual personal engagement— riding a school bus with children to ensure their safe transit—is replicated by tens of thousands of teachers who go far beyond their job descriptions to assist pupils in areas that have little to do with raising test scores but everything to do with creating environments appropriate for learning. You might find your own aspirations reflected in Jeff's goals and in his quest to promote learning that is meaningful for children. Or you might have found a kindred spirit in Grace or Maggie, who found ways to document pupil behavior and learning that turned problematic situations into positive outcomes. In each case, you may find your own thought processes mirrored in the continual inner reflection of the teachers—which sometimes becomes truly obsessive in its intensity—precisely because you are dealing with young children who are entrusted to your care and often have little recourse beyond your decisions about their lives.

Each of these cases to a certain extent is bounded by its singularity and specificity. And while anchoring illustrations are important, it is necessary at this juncture to try to derive general principles from the cases, which, combined with research findings, can help us to articulate a theory of mindful teaching and accompanying practices—a task to which we turn in the next chapter.

NOTE

1. Pseudonyms have been used for selected teachers and schools and for all students to protect confidentiality.

CHAPTER 4

The Seven Synergies
of Mindful Teaching

I N THIS CHAPTER we build on our foregoing descriptions and a review of research to elaborate in greater detail what we mean by mindful teaching and to suggest affiliated practices for teachers. By doing so, we seek to assist educators by providing a new conceptual frame for understanding our common challenges and opportunities. In addition, we wish to spark and extend a conversation about mindfulness and its relevance and utility to education. Our discussion is organized around what we describe as seven qualities, or, more exactly, *seven synergies of mindful teaching*. Since we do not believe that mindful teaching can address all of the problems currently challenging American education, we describe the limitations of mindful teaching through an elaboration of *three tensions of mindful teaching*.

THE SEVEN SYNERGIES

The term *synergy* originated in medicine and anthropology and conveys the idea that latent resources can be marshaled and released when individual actions are placed in right relationships with others to create a positive dynamism that is renewable and more than the sum of its parts (Benedict, 1934). Charles Payne (2008) has commented that one of the challenges facing urban education is that in many ways individual actions actually add up to *less* than the sum of their parts. This is because so many relationships—including those between adults—are riddled with mistrust. If this is indeed the case, then a countervailing set of beliefs and practices that nourish trust and connectedness would seem to be warranted. Following our seminars and accompanying practices, we studied and reflected upon our findings and attempted to ascertain whether there were any underlying patterns, or theories of action that could be derived from them, that could be interpreted in light of other research to espouse

Figure 4.1. The Seven Synergies of Mindful Teaching

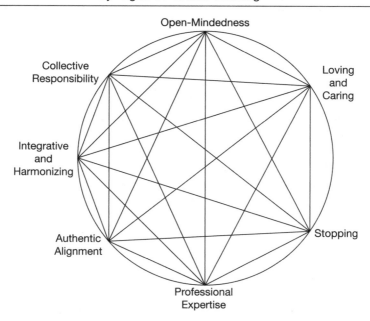

a theory of mindful teaching. We scoured through our tape transcriptions of seminar meetings and our notes from our interviews with seminar participants, and then coded the concerns and solutions that recurred repeatedly. We then clustered those concerns together when they bore a conceptual resemblance to one another, shared our findings with seminar participants, and refined our articulation of each idea through additional elaboration and clarification. Through this process we identified *seven synergies of mindful teaching* that are visually represented in Figure 4.1.

Why is synergy an appropriate term to use? In opening his pedagogical classic entitled *Experience and Education*, John Dewey (1938) began by noting that "mankind likes to think in terms of extreme opposites. It is given to formulating its beliefs in terms of *Either–Ors*, between which it recognizes no intermediate possibilities" (p. 17). Dewey's (1916) entire philosophy of education is based upon the overcoming of such oppositions or dualisms in an effort to establish harmony and balance in education and to develop new capacities. In this way Dewey's thinking foreshadows the seven synergies of mindful teaching that we have derived from our anchoring illustrations. The importance of open-mindedness, commitment to the whole child, and educators as lifelong learners—the cornerstones of Dewey's philosophy—are all reflected in mindful teaching. Not coincidentally, Dewey's philosophy of education met with great popular resonance among Asian scholars, who saw in his effort at overcoming dualisms many affinities with their own native traditions of Confucianism, Taoism, and Buddhism (Frisina, 2002).

OPEN-MINDEDNESS

Of all of these, the first and most important synergy is a commitment to *open-mindedness*. In our first anchoring illustration, Olivia's perspective grew from that of a defensive teacher into that of an educator who came to understand that administrators suffer under their own sets of pressures, many of which are beyond their control. Virtually all of Ellen Langer's (1989, 1997) work on mindfulness is based on the finding that learners in all kinds of situations quickly fall prey to ingrained habitual modes of acting and believing that prevent them from being open to new kinds of information that call for new responses.

Is it wrong for teachers to curse and shout at students and to support parents when they are authoritarian with their children? Most of us would say yes. But education is much more complicated than this. In his research Pedro Noguera (2008) has discussed his finding that African American students report that they would rather have teachers who hold them to high standards, even if this involves some yelling for emphasis, than teachers who are apathetic and disengaged. In dangerous urban neighborhoods authoritarian parenting can be more predictive of student success than other approaches because there is such a small margin for error (Benard, 2006).

John Stuart Mill (1931) once wrote about education that "of all of the many sided-things, it is the one with the most sides" (p. 32). Plato's *Republic*, Confucius's *Analects*, and classics of Indian philosophy and theology such as the *Upanishads* and the *Bhagavad-Gita* all embrace the polyvalence and elusive qualities of education. But only rarely do we allow this complexity to emerge. Complexity needs to be enabled, discussed, and debated. Teachers like Jeff need school structures and cultures that will enable this complexity so that they can come to know and teach their pupils better. Being open-minded allows us to engage our pupils as they are now, not just as we might want them to be.

We can't escape sloganeering in education, but too often we let slogan systems substitute for deep reflection. Even our distinctions between alienated and mindful teaching should be called into question, because it is likely that at least a moment of alienation or uncertainty can be the prelude for inquiry and for deeper learning about one's assumptions and

biases. Many teachers might assume that having a calm and quiet classroom is a necessary part of mindful teaching, but some research on children with attention deficit hyperactivity disorder indicates that playing
rock music while children performed an academic task helped to increase
their attentiveness to the task (Cripe, 1986). So the first ethic of mindful
teaching is open-mindedness or what Thich Nhat Hanh (1998) calls "non-
attachment from views" (p. 17).

Caring

The second synergy of mindful teaching relates to a disposition of *caring*, or even *loving*, at the heart of teaching. Renee rode the school bus
with children from Roxbury not because she was anxious that China
and India pose an economic challenge to the United States, but because
she experienced on a daily basis the connections between the children's
learning in school and their environments outside of school. Karyn didn't
worry about her "runner" just because Cecilia was distracting other children from learning. She worried about her because the girl was in difficult straits and her longings for her mother and a better future elicited
the strongest of emotions that were both educational and maternal in
nature. When teachers in our seminar worried that children on individual educational plans were being short-changed by not receiving legally
mandated services as a result of their learning disabilities, the teachers
weren't just upset that their schools weren't following protocol. Perhaps
most troubling at all, when teachers saw their very own colleagues mis-
treating children through a constant stream of verbal abuse—yelling at
them to shut up or insulting their intelligence—they worried deeply that
educators were neglecting an ethic of caring that they viewed as the very
heart and soul of the teaching profession.

Nel Noddings (1992, 2001) argued that education without a disposition of caring at the center must remain a hollow and ultimately trun-
cated enterprise that inevitably will produce a reaction of skepticism and
justifiable resistance among learners. Jim Scheurich (1998), in a study
of high-achieving schools serving low-income students of color, found
that educators' explanations of their success with students often were
predicated upon what they rather prosaically described as their love of
the students. Recently scholars have engaged in heated debate with one
another about the complexities involved in measuring educators' dispositions and their impact on pupil learning, and there is no gainsaying
the difficulties of this undertaking for psychologists and psychometricians
(Borko, Liston, & Whitcomb, 2007). But however daunting it may be to
operationalize and then measure the impact of dispositions on learning,

it nonetheless remains true that none of our six anchoring illustrations make any sense without recourse to the emotional longings and aspirations that the teachers have for their pupils. Cutting off discussions about these longings—trivializing them as romantic, impractical, or even anti-intellectual—hardly works if education is to manifest itself as a humanistic and humanizing enterprise.

Stopping

In an institutional setting in which "innovative overload" and "repetitive change syndrome" have become normalized as routine forms of everyday life, the third synergy of mindful teaching is simply *stopping*. And then stopping again. And then again.

It might seem ridiculous to imagine that simply stopping could be described as emancipatory. We are socialized to believe that being busy is a virtue. If this is the case, how could it be that Megan and her pupils had a different experience—and what might that mean for a theory of mindful teaching?

Since theory is effective only up to a point, and then experience is more generative, we ask you to try this: *stop right now*. Put this book down, assume a posture reflecting your inherent worth and dignity as a human being, and close your eyes for a few minutes. Observe calmly and nonjudgmentally the various images, recollections, projects, and longings that surface in your mind. Adapt an inner attitude of compassion and reverence toward yourself as a sentient being experiencing all of the suffering and cravings that sentient beings are subject to. Then direct that inner attitude toward your students, starting with those whom you find the easiest to relate to and gradually including those whom you find more adversarial or challenging. Then allow your attention to return to yourself and your aspirations to enable each of your pupils to learn and reach his or her full potential. Finally, reflect upon the change in your consciousness at the beginning, in the middle, and at the end of this small mindfulness exercise.

Furthermore, allow yourself time for this exercise. If you are new to meditation, you might enter into the exercise and begin with simply 10 minutes of contemplative practice. Over time you might wish to expand upon it, learning about yourself and bringing a more open frame of mind to your interactions with your students when you next encounter them.

With inner peace and concentration more possibilities open up for modifying your action than when you are hurried and stressed. This finding is reinforced over and over again by a wide variety of research in meditation practices and neuroplasticity (Austin, 1998; Begley, 2007; Siegel,

2007). You can't achieve inner balance if you are always rushing and engulfed in projects. In such a context, you cannot be sensitive to your emotional and intellectual responses to events, and your responses to all that comes your way as a teacher can be only reactive rather than informed by reflective judgment. While formal meditation might be an optimal way of stopping and re-centering yourself, busy teachers cannot always do this, so it is important to recall that "meditation can be very informal" (Hahn, 2005, p. 16) and, with the right frame of mind, can occur in the midst of everyday life. So the third synergy of mindful teaching is stopping and taking an inner account of what is transpiring, and not allowing yourself to be rushed into actions that you might regret later.

Professional Expertise

Of course, it is all very well and good to be open-minded, loving, and to stop and think as educators. But what good does this avail students if one doesn't know the subject matter one is teaching, has a limited range of vocabulary for conveying ideas to students, and makes no effort to keep abreast of recent research findings or reforms in the profession? We cannot emphasize sufficiently the fourth synergy of mindful teaching, which is *professional expertise*. Throughout our seminar discussions teachers expressed exasperation with colleagues who not only were disinterested in educational research, but were actively hostile toward those who sought to share it either informally in the teachers' room or more formally by guiding the deliberations of instructional leadership teams. Seminar participants were enraged by promotions that were awarded to teachers and administrators on the basis of seniority rather than professional achievements. And they felt degraded when they attended professional development workshops that advocated instructional reforms without sharing evidence that the reforms were effective or without discussing the costs as well as the benefits of the reforms.

Seminar participants developed their sense of professional expertise through multiple venues. Some focused on raising pupil achievement through rigorous drill and assessment activities that they alternated with complex interdisciplinary units that kept their classrooms novel and exciting. Others team-taught education courses with professors at Boston College and opened up their classrooms for research with student teachers, as Grace Napolitano did with Marlene Gomez in one of our anchoring illustrations. Others pursued certification through the National Board for Professional Teaching Standards and used participation in the seminars and contributions to this book as evidence of continual learning and growth in the profession. Still others took on hybrid roles as literacy or math coaches in their own buildings, and by switching roles, discovered that working with reluctant and disengaged colleagues is much harder in reality than it appears on paper. Professional expertise takes many forms in schools today, and when encouraged by principals through distributed leadership models, is highly correlated with gains in pupil achievement (Harris, 2008; Spillane, 2006).

Authentic Alignment

Given the complexity of professional expertise, it follows that the fifth synergy of mindful teaching is *authentic alignment*. Educators hear endless amounts today about the need to align their instruction with district standards, professional association standards, state standards, and state curriculum frameworks. The amount of time that goes into establishing charts aligning different standards with one another and with curriculum frameworks and tests is prodigious. In many cases, elementary school teachers are required by their principals, districts, or states to write the instructional objectives for each subject area to be covered—reading, writing, math, science, social studies, and art—on the board at the beginning of each day. They also are required to keep lesson plan books with all of the state standards linked to each activity every day. Finally, for certain subjects schools are mandated to teach a certain number of minutes every week.

When viewed as helpful indicators to be considered by novice teachers, such admonitions can provide a useful frame of reference for planning instructional activities. When considered from the point of view of experienced professionals, however, an excessive concern with alignment can rob teachers of opportunities to adjust their instruction to teach students at their actual level of understanding or to create exciting lessons with novel kinds of group structures and purposeful independent study. Teachers need to ask themselves whether their teaching approaches are aligned with their own understanding of teaching as a profession, and when dissonance occurs, they need opportunities to reframe their activities.

Recent research by Howard Gardner, Mihalyi Csikszentmihalyi, and William Damon (2001) puts such authentic alignment between ethical conviction and action at the core of professional fulfillment and efficacy. Indeed, without such undergirding ethical principles, it would appear that a profession cannot even exist, because, at its core, professional status relies on implicit social trust between professionals and the public that the professionals are indeed legitimate and acting in the public interest.

When professionals neglect ethics, they undermine their own integrity and credibility, and the accompanying public skepticism is a necessary and altogether unavoidable consequence.

Integration and Harmonization

A sixth synergy of mindful teaching is that it is *integrative and harmonizing*. Michael Fullan (2001, p. 31) has used the phrase "dynamic conservatism" to convey the way in which expert teachers incorporate new practices into their repertoire without abandoning previous strategies. While some scholarship (Cohen, 1990) has decried the manner in which teachers incorporate innovative practices—such as constructivist mathematics, for example—into anterior, more traditional approaches, our perspective is less dualistic. Reformers need to be less hurried and more respectful of teachers' practices, even those that are traditional and might seem quaint in an age of continual technological breakthroughs. Some of the older teaching practices and pastoral approaches that were maintained by Catholic schools, for example, have been vindicated, while public schools careened from one reform approach to another (Bryk, Lee, & Holland, 1993). Yet public school teachers such as Grace and Maggie have found ways to blend what some would consider to be conservative approaches—such as applied behavioral analysis or systematic phonics— with a broader repertoire of personalized and progressive pedagogies. Mindful teaching, we suggest, skillfully blends the old and the new.

Collective Responsibility

The seventh synergy of mindful teaching is *collective responsibility*. In high-achieving Finland, there is no term for "accountability" in education, and the public has rejected the notion because it undermines the shared nature of the enterprise. Significantly, Finland has the smallest achievement gap between the rich and poor of any of the nations measured on the Program for International Student Assessment tests. The very notion that an educator like Renee would find herself compelled to ride a school bus so that her pupils would arrive safely at school in the morning would strike the more collectivist Finns as an abrogation of the broader societal obligation to children and to educators, who are regarded with the highest of esteem (Hargreaves, Halász, & Pont, 2008).

We prefer the Finnish understanding of collective responsibility to the practice of accountability that has been favored by Anglo-American reformers over the past 20 years. For American educators, and for the broader public as well, this needs to entail a renewal of civic activism—whether through community organizing, social movements, or hybrid public–private partnerships—to reduce the dramatic increases in social inequality that have developed in the past quarter century and to close academic achievement gaps (Anyon, 2005; Oakes, Rogers, & Lipton, 2006; Peterman, 2008). Teachers have a special role to play here as those civic professionals who are entrusted with the education of the young, so the transformation of accountability systems into more community-based, informative, and learning-enhancing kinds of assessment and transparency must be part of a broader change strategy for the years to come (Murrell, 2001). If we are successful, we will be able to move beyond the current period toward what we hope will be a new era of poststandardization (Hargreaves & Shirley, 2008).

The seven synergies of mindful teaching—open-mindedness, caring, stopping, expertise, authentic alignment, integration, and collective responsibility—provide important principles for developing and improving teaching. But it would be illusory to advocate that these seven synergies even come close to providing a toolkit or recipe list for pedagogical decision making. Each of the synergies has to be brought into a mutually supportive relationship with all of the others, and they become useless or even destructive if they are communicated in a tone of voice or attitude of dismissal that is wounding and degrading to others. The synergies of mindful teaching are not about preaching and proselytizing, but about the responsibilities of each and every one of us to adjust our own behaviors in light of our highest principles. And even then the seven synergies are complemented by the triple tensions of mindful teaching.

THE TRIPLE TENSIONS OF MINDFUL TEACHING

The first tension of mindful teaching is *the tension between contemplation and action*. To be mindful, one must take time to become attuned to and reflective about what is transpiring. One can do this through incorporating formal meditation into one's everyday life, through keeping a journal of one's experiences, or through prayer. Students also can be brought into these processes in ways that contribute to a calm and focused classroom environment (Lantieri, 2008; Payton et al., 2008).

Beneficial as these contemplative activities are, in our seminar discussions teachers continually struggled with issues of time management and the day-to-day pressures of their professional lives in schools. Meditation CDs that we gave the teachers were received appreciatively, but with the press of events they would go unused by several of the teachers, only

Figure 4.2. The Triple Tensions of Mindful Teaching

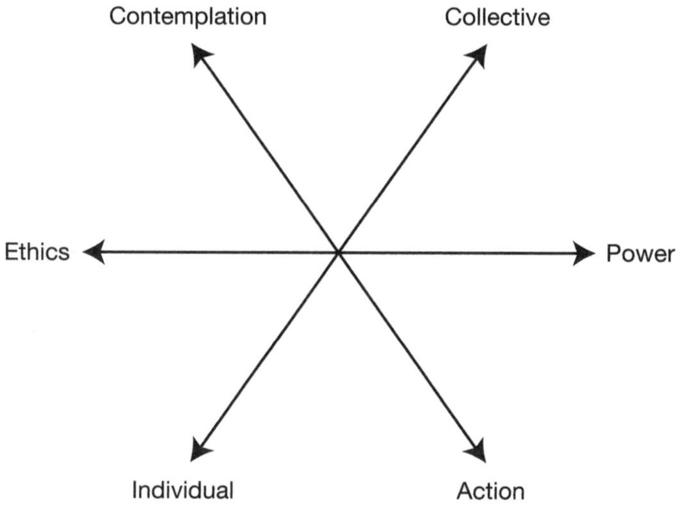

rarely becoming part of formal daily practices. When teachers like Olivia, Renee, and Jeff took on extra projects and tasks that truly served their pupils, that extra time took away from restorative time they needed to shelter and attend to their private lives. Teachers would promise themselves that they would stop work each evening by 7:00 but still be going for hours afterward.

As seminar leaders, we did not know how to resolve the tensions that teachers experienced between the needs of their pupils and their own needs for well-rounded private lives. Many reformers would argue that of course the needs of the pupils come first—but then the same reformers seem puzzled by the horrific rates of teachers leaving the profession. Too many of our seminar discussions came to involve questions of how much longer individuals could remain in the urban classroom. Our role became that of compassionate allies who sought to establish a precarious balance between the needs of the pupils for learning and the needs of the teacher for a profession that invites not 3 years of idealism followed by burnout and exit, but long-term sustainable growth and fulfillment.

The second tension of mindful teaching is *the tension between ethics and power*. Mindful ethics require us to treat others as their own ends and not as instruments for securing our own status or privilege. Here is a point of convergence between Western and Eastern ethics, as expressed, for example, by Immanuel Kant's categorical imperative on the one hand and the Lotus Sutra on the other. As teachers we need continually to review our decisions and the tone and manner in which we enact them in terms of their contributions to an atmosphere of deep respect and compassion for others. We need to know when to speak up to advocate for our pupils when they do not have the power to advocate for themselves.

One incident in the life of one of our seminar participants is illustrative here. Frank is a third-grade teacher who works in an elementary school in which the children have only 20 minutes of recess a week—and this is contingent upon the children demonstrating good behavior and completing all of their homework. Many of the children live in neighborhoods that have experienced escalating youth violence in recent years, so their parents do not allow them to play outside when they are home from school. Emboldened by Mindful Teacher seminar discussions about ethics and advocacy, Frank spoke up at a school staff meeting and argued for more recess time for the children each week. The next morning his principal showed up in his classroom unannounced to conduct an assessment of his teaching.

Frank learned that advocacy for students by teachers can lead to heightened surveillance of teachers by administrators. Yet this second tension exists because an excessive concern with ethics can lead to disengagement from politics. For if one is overly moralistic and neglects to acknowledge the realities of power, one can withdraw from the public space altogether, disdaining it as inherently suspect and almost beneath one's dignity. Such a stance is dangerous in any democracy, which depends upon civic engagement to enhance worthy goals related to social justice and human rights. Our project was grant-funded, which was not so important in regard to the small stipends it provided teachers but enormously significant in terms of the institutional imprimaturs of Boston College and the Boston Public Schools. Making sure that others knew about the grant through a Web site (www.mindfulteacher.com), conference presentations, and even this book itself also was important to nourish our ongoing learning as a professional community and to enable others to engage with and critique our work.

The third tension of mindful teaching is *the tension between the individual and the collective.* As teachers we need colleagues who will support us during tough times and challenge us when we display errors in judgment, which can range from speaking harshly to a child or acting rudely to a parent or another colleague. Ideally, we are all constantly involved in providing one another with mutual support. Yet could it be the case that educators sometimes are subject to groupthink, and that in our praiseworthy goals to be supportive of our colleagues, we sometimes put this ahead of our students' interests and needs?

An important body of research (Campbell, 2005; Lima, 2001) indicates that this is indeed the case, documenting the many ways in which educators are conflict averse, preferring silence to commentary in the face of injustices (Rusch, 2005). This professional culture of looking the other way—even in the face of egregious injustices to children—has to be engaged directly and overcome. Therefore, even though an important part of mindful teaching entails valorizing calmness and concentration, mindful teaching cannot mean passivity or acquiescence in contexts of injustice. It must rather call forth civil courage and even bold confrontations. Crucial here is the spirit and tenor of the confrontations. For it is precisely when we are most motivated by high moral purpose that we can be most prone to demonizing and dehumanizing others with opposing perspectives and values. And it is precisely for this reason that the road to hell so often has been paved, stone by stone, with good intentions gone awry.

CODA

The seven synergies of mindful teaching provide purpose, direction, and cohesion to mindful teaching as a set of pedagogical principles and practices. The triple tensions, however, remind us that those synergies cannot pretend to be prescriptive in all situations and contexts. Schools will continue to struggle with abused and abusive administrators, and children whose parents are depressed, in jail, or on drugs. School funding streams will go up and down in response to economic boom and bust. Promising innovations, even when they yield excellent results, will be phased out when foundation heads change and new leaders want to put their own imprint on the programs they are funding. Even in well-funded schools with talented educators and strong community support, the very frailty and unpredictability of the human condition will lead to pupils who drop out, staff who quit in the middle of the school year, and administrators who become bored by intractable problems with teachers and children. For all of these reasons—and for many more—we need something more than mindful teaching. We need *mindful teacher leadership*—the subject of our final chapter.

CHAPTER 5

Mindful Teacher Leadership

ONE OF THE greatest challenges for teacher leadership today was formulated many years ago by Michael Huberman (1993), who found that when teachers reflected on their careers at the stage of retirement, those who reported the most fulfilment were those who had sheltered themselves from larger school reform initiatives. Those with the most frustration were those who had tried to change system-level policies and had been thwarted in their efforts. This finding, which subsequently has become known as the "Huberman paradox" (Little & Bartlett, 2002, p. 352), and its ramifications have troubled teacher leaders and educational change advocates ever since. For if teachers do not step forth and begin to lead change processes, can teaching ever truly become a profession? Without scaffolded opportunities for teachers to lead, are teachers forever doomed to fall back to the unholy trinity of conservatism, presentism, and privatism described in Chapter 1?

Our findings from the Mindful Teacher project are cautiously optimistic on this account. When Lortie wrote *Schoolteacher* in the 1970s and when Huberman conducted his studies in the 1980s, there was little momentum to foster teachers as researchers or as leaders. Yet in the years since, there has been a sea change in education. While efforts to develop teachers as researchers and leaders often are subject to the usual spasmodic, stop-and-go patterns endemic in educational change, we now are in an altogether different era. School districts all over the nation support teachers' professional learning communities. Teachers are acquiring opportunities for differentiated roles such as literacy or math coaches in their buildings, and the revolution in information technology has enabled teachers to network with colleagues from across the country and indeed around the world on everything from effective teaching strategies for autistic children to multicultural education. An increasing amount of educational change is transnational in scope, enabling educators to learn from their colleagues not just down the hall or in a neighboring district, but also from other nations in locations as far removed as Finland, Japan, and Singapore.

In addition to these exciting new developments supporting teacher leadership in schools, scholars have documented that an older "heroic" model of school leadership based on a single charismatic principal does not fit our contemporary situation, for several reasons. The first of these is that while a few charismatic individuals with strong leadership skills can be found from time to time, they are not nearly available enough in large enough numbers in proportion to the number of schools in struggling circumstances (Hargreaves & Fink, 2006). Second, the sheer magnitude of a principal's job has ballooned so much in recent years that few educators are interested in becoming principals (Cusick, 2002; Hewitt, Pijanowski, Carmine, & Denny, 2008). This reality of "leadership in crisis" (Harris, 2008, p. 16) has created new pressures within schools to redistribute power and authority by viewing leadership not so much as the attribute of a single individual but rather as a network constituted by the interactions of administrators, teachers, and their situation (Spillane & Diamond, 2007). Third, it turns out that upon closer examination, many highly visible leaders with apparent charisma actually turn out to be skilled developers of their teachers' capacity to lead, so that a more "distributed" model of leadership has been put into practice than is evident at first glance (Harris, 2008; Spillane, 2006).

The pressurized environment facing principals and other administrators is an important, but not the only, reason for the growing interest in and practice of teacher leadership. Scholars have found that schools in which teachers provide more influential leadership are considered by the teachers themselves to be more effective, and student engagement is impacted significantly and positively by teacher leadership (Leithwood, Jantzi, & Steinbach, 1999). Fears that empowered teachers might lead to more adversarial relationships with administrators do not appear to be validated by the research, because that empowerment seems to accompany a rise in communicative competence within a school that increases teacher efficacy (Ingersoll, 2003). For most teachers, leadership is not expressed through random activities, but rather those that are focused on improving student learning (Murphy, Goldring, & Porter, 2006).

THREE LEVELS OF MINDFUL TEACHER LEADERSHIP

The vast majority of the teacher leadership that we documented and catalyzed through the Mindful Teacher seminars can be described as *microlevel* interventions. When Jeff made the book on El Salvador for Gregorio, when Grace worked patiently and steadfastly with Miguel to help him to modify his behavior so that he could learn better, and when Karyn modified her classroom to contain Cecilia's "running," each teacher exemplified the trial-and-error learning by gathering data and collaborative reflection that are at the heart of all good teaching. These were classroom-level changes that demonstrated the power of good teachers to assess the learning environment they had created among their students and to shift dimensions of their day-to-day instruction and interactions to support learning.

Yet Mindful Teacher participants also demonstrated *mesolevel* leadership, especially in our seminar settings. One of the most striking findings from the seminars was that teachers continually discovered that a practice that they thought was districtwide turned out to be peculiar to the culture of their own buildings. Teachers helped one another to understand the role and power of school site councils, instructional leadership teams, and whole-school improvement plans. When violence spiked in the community, a teacher strike was narrowly averted, or when mathematics and literacy coaches were cut due to a fiscal crisis, teachers continually were able to assist one another to learn what district policy was and what decisions appeared to have been made (sometimes without teacher involvement) in their buildings.

On the one hand, almost all of what we have come to call *mindful teacher leadership* happens at the microlevel. Teachers want kids to learn, and our focus each and every day isn't on adults, but on the children and young people who crowd our classrooms eager to be engaged and to thrive. We know teachers also can benefit from mesolevel activities like the Mindful Teacher seminars that allow us to share and spread knowledge within and across schools. But occasionally teachers have opportunities to move not only beyond their schools and their districts, but also beyond their states and even their nations. When teachers not only attend conferences, but also present their work to one another and receive validation from others in professional settings, the result can be a powerful sense of catharsis and lateral learning. Teachers can then take what they have learned from these *macrolevel* experiences back to their schools to inform their instructional practices and teacher leadership in their districts. Just as is the case for other professionals, these opportunities to step outside of the classroom and garner new insights from others engaged in similar processes can be decisive catalysts for professional renewal and growth.

LIZ MACDONALD: GROWING INTO TEACHER LEADERSHIP

Back in the spring of 2005 when Dennis and I were writing our proposal for the Mindful Teacher project and envisioning what supports we might offer the teachers, I felt most adamant about including funding for teachers to attend professional conferences, which was an uncommon practice among most of the teachers I knew in the district. Due to the partnership work that I had done with Boston College, I was afforded the opportunity to not only attend but to present at several national conferences, including the American Educational Research Association, the National Council of Teachers of English, and the Holmes Partnership. Upon entering this previously unknown world of roundtable discussions, symposiums, and panel presentations, my educational knowledge was vastly expanded, yet I became even more alienated in my school building. How could I go back and tell my colleagues that I just spent 3 luxurious days in an exciting city listening to the most recent research, networking with educational leaders, and discussing the politics of school reform over a nice dinner with professors from schools of education?

I can vividly remember hearing an opening presentation about the recently signed No Child Left Behind Act at a conference in Washington, DC. Six months later I attended a whole-school meeting during which the district first mentioned anything about NCLB and its enormous implications for our teaching. On the one hand, I felt incredibly fortunate to have my professional life enriched. On the other hand, I was outraged that my colleagues at the ground level were not part of the conversations at these conferences.

In our third year of the Mindful Teacher project the prospect of sharing our work with other teachers became a possibility when we learned about the upcoming International Conference of Teacher Research to be held at Bank Street College in New York City. The seminar teachers enthusiastically met up on a cold winter's night after a day of teaching to collectively write a proposal and send it off a day before the deadline. After we received a congratulatory acceptance letter from Cindy Ballenger, ICTR's Program Chair, the teachers' excitement mounted. What would we say? Who would be there? How would we travel?

Dennis then informed me that he would not be able to accompany us due to a prior personal commitment that weekend. Of course, I knew that this was his way of cutting the cord and allowing us all to exercise our professional expertise. What I did not realize at the time was how momentous this decision was and the tremendous impact it would have on the teachers, including myself.

The night before our presentation we met up in the hotel lounge to finalize our presentation and make arrangements for the day. As the last member of our group of seven entered the lounge upon arrival in the city, we all cheered! We were hugging each other with an air of both anxiousness and exhilaration. "I can't believe we are actually here," we said to one another. "This is so cool!"

I myself was in awe of the fact that I was now the leader of this Mindful Teacher group and they were looking to me for guidance about presenting at an international conference. The next morning we took cabs over to the West Side on our journey to the conference. For most of us, this was going to be the first time both attending and presenting at a conference.

Once we arrived, we listened to the keynote address by Vivian Paley. Entitled "Looking for Magpie: How to Locate Your Voice as Teacher and Researcher," Paley's words resonated with us, especially when she said that "the teacher is alone in the classroom looking for his or her voice." Here we were presenting about the Mindful Teacher, and we knew that sense of loneliness was such a big part of the alienated teaching that we all had experienced.

After breaking up to attend a variety of presentations during the first session, we met up for lunch, where teachers shared their excitement and nervousness about our upcoming symposium. I told the teachers not to be disappointed if our session was not well attended, reminding them that this was our first public engagement and we might not attract a large audience. At the same time, I tried to speak to everyone I met to encourage them to come to our presentation.

Contrary to my prediction, our session was jam-packed with people still entering minutes after we began. Many of the audience had no space left to sit but the floor! We had divided ourselves up so that each of us was able to share the origin, purpose, and themes of the Mindful Teacher. The energy from the crowd motivated the presenters and I felt pride as I watched my colleagues take over with ease and confidence. Many lingered after the presentation, asking the participants questions, exchanging emails, and commenting on the need for such a group at their school or partnership school.

One of the highlights of the day came when Ann Lieberman, co-author of a book on teacher leadership (Lieberman & Miller, 2004) that we read for discussion at one of our Mindful Teacher seminars, came over to talk with us. I previously had met Ann at a conference in Chicago and discussed the project's work over breakfast during which she offered some helpful advice about teacher leadership. More important, Ann validated and appreciated my own work as a teacher leader, giving me the assurance to continue my work. The teachers were blown away that Ann Lieberman was before them chatting informally about the conference and their work as teacher researchers. At that moment I truly could feel their excitement and was happy to see them now part of the conversation. We ended the day with a celebratory dinner back on the East Side where we were staying, but the real revelry has manifested itself in a variety of ways since that day.

Presenting at the conference as a group of teachers without a university member present gave us all a great sense of agency along with an affirmation that what teachers think, does matter. The group had an opportunity to interact with student teachers, teachers, administrators, professors, and researchers who were open-minded, caring, and able to slow down to think and reflect upon their practices and the current policies in education. Jeff later shared with me that he "wished we could take everyone from this conference and put them on an island and all teach together." The insular world of the teacher's classroom, school building, and district had been expanded to one in which each of us could express our thoughts and opinions without fearing any ramifications. We were able to recognize ourselves as teacher leaders who could share our experiences with colleagues from not just around the country but even around the globe.

We don't know whether the teachers at the conference who shared their enthusiasm with us know just what an impact their support had on us. We returned home eager to carry on our work to another stage. We applied for and received another 3-year grant from the Boston Collaborative Fellows program to continue the Mindful Teacher seminars. This time, we stretched our work across the city to a "superintendent's school" in Dorchester named Russell Elementary. A superintendent's school is one that is identified for special assistance in the district because of its low test score results.

While the idea was that the Mindful Teacher project would be helping a struggling and underperforming school, something else happened. In October 2008 I learned that my own school, as part of a districtwide cost-saving measure, was to be closed and consolidated into a nearby middle school, along with another neighborhood elementary school. While we had known at my school that our enrollments were low and the economy seemed to be getting worse and worse by the minute, the news still was devastating. Over the summer one of my colleagues had been chosen to be our new principal, and we had spent months planning how we were going to all collaborate and plan together to make the new year better than ever.

What to do? I took the issue to the Mindful Teacher seminar. It turns out that the participating teachers from Russell Elementary, who had many more years in the district than I did, had lots of great advice for my colleagues and me about how to guide this process. They pointed out potential advantages with becoming part of a K–8 school and named all kinds of programs and services that we could tap into. They also encouraged us to speak up so that we wouldn't just be on the receiving end of bad news but could shape the environment in ways that would help our kids in the new building. With the help of my Mindful Teacher colleagues I mustered the courage to speak before the Boston School Committee, urging them to let teachers be part of the whole transition process.

How did mindfulness enter into this? We knew that the Boston Public Schools were facing a financial crisis. We knew that our school's neighborhood of Allston–Brighton was undergoing rapid demographic change and that families with children had decreased. Superintendent Carol Johnson had to cut costs somewhere in light of the dire financial situation, and our school seemed like an obvious candidate.

Mindfulness entered in because our first impulse to attack the district leadership and defend our school really wouldn't help in light of the financial crisis. Superintendent Johnson had a tough job and it wouldn't help anything to make it tougher. So our role was to ask for real inclusion and a real voice in the process. Our role was to make sure that our kids wouldn't get short-changed, but would have a chance to thrive in a building that was first built and then set up for middle school kids.

Please, teacher friends and colleagues who are reading this book, don't think that we are saying that we have all of the answers! When I think back to some of my dark days of teaching prior to the Mindful Teacher project when I was on the verge of leaving the profession, feelings of alienation, failure, and unhappiness immediately resurface in my memory. Since that time, pacing guides, high-stakes accountability, and taxing students have not disappeared. There are still days that I teeter on despair and feel like giving up the fight to educate all children because of the external factors beyond my control.

It is at those times that I rely most heavily on one of basic tenets of mindful teaching: stopping. I stop to contemplate why I teach and am reminded like many of you reading this now: I teach because I care. I care about all of the children and especially about those who require support, guidance, and stability both emotionally and academically and for whom school is the only place they find it. I care about the quality of education of urban school children who too often have had their standards lowered. I care about the families who do not have the human or social capital to seek out the best resources for themselves and their children. I care about my fellow educators who have fought long and hard for the rights of teachers and have weathered many a storm of reform. Some of them have done this for as many years as I have lived! And I care about the profession of teaching and the future it holds for all of the young, bright, and fervent individuals who have the power to legitimize the importance of good teaching. And then I reach out to those around me who care too.

REACHING OUT

As we now come to the close of this book, we hope that you have acquired a number of tools for thinking about how you might reach out to others if you are inspired to work mindfully as an educator. We hasten to reiterate a theme that has come up again and again in the foregoing pages: *For any of these tools to work, they have to be adapted wisely to your own situation.* To make this adaptation effective you have to draw upon the full repertoire of your professional expertise, consulting your experience, the range of available data, and situational factors such as competing reforms, student demographic trends, and the impact of the current economic recession on resource allocation. Only if these tools are mediated by open-minded and caring educators who take their prior experiences and skills seriously and who see teaching as a *vocation* (from the Latin *vocare* or "call," in the sense of a "calling") will the tools be able to realize the humanistic purposes for which they are intended.

To summarize some of our key points made throughout this volume, we now review our *eightfold strategies*, *seven synergies*, and *triple tensions* of mindful teaching. The strategies are presented again here in the event that you would like to establish a similar seminar structure in your school or district. If you do decide to adapt the structures to your own context, we ask that you recall that it took us several years until our structures solidified. Choosing the right kind of incidents to discuss as part of selective vulnerability, for example, requires a finely tuned sense of just what seminar participants are ready for: too much vulnerability can overwhelm participants with the sense that a crisis has careened out of control, while too little vulnerability can suggest that the seminar leaders are reluctant to share their own struggles with the group. Allowing the group multiple opportunities to help to shape the evolving conversation, and modulating the tenor and direction of group reflection over time, will be of great importance in assuring that the seminar serves all of the participants well.

Likewise, the introduction of formal meditation practices requires great sensitivity to the cultures and personalities of seminar participants. We began with taped 10-minute guided meditations led by Jon Kabat-Zinn and made sure that participants inexperienced with meditation had plenty of time to discuss the difficulties that they encountered with calming and focusing their minds. Seminar leaders need to be sensitive to the different religious perspectives of seminar participants, and need to know that even if the leaders do not think that meditation raises any issues in terms of participants' religious beliefs, participants may have other points of view on the matter.

Our eightfold strategies for a seminar setting are supported by seven synergies of mindful teaching—a value orientation that evolved over the years of the seminars and resonated with our teachers. The seven synergies must be interdependent on one another. None is complete without a relationship of dynamic equilibrium with each of the other coordinates. One can't intend to be *loving* and yet neglect one's *professional expertise* as an educator. One can't claim to be *open-minded* and yet fail to *stop* and consider

---

THE EIGHTFOLD STRATEGIES

1. Create a safe and trusting climate for sharing teachers' *pressing concerns*, as soon as possible after teachers arrive in the seminar setting;
2. Encourage openness through *selective vulnerability* by choosing a topic of individual concern identified by a teacher leader in advance that others can relate to based on similar experiences with their own students or colleagues;
3. Bring *scholarly research* to bear on a given topic through careful study and preparation outside of the seminar setting;
4. Practice *formal meditation,* both in the seminar setting and at home, to calm and focus the mind and to be open and attuned to new information;
5. Enable small-group work on the *psychological intrusions* that arise during formal meditation to bring forth the range of concerns preoccupying seminar participants;
6. Use a *tuning protocol* to go deeper on an issue of special importance to an individual, especially when the topic is time-sensitive and the individual would appreciate concentrated attention as soon as possible;
7. Enable *extended debriefing* on both the tuning protocol and the entire session, including time to discuss readings and activities for the next seminar.
8. Establish *mindfulness assignments* that assist teachers to focus on discrete domains of instruction that easily can escape our awareness and yet can enable us to understand our students better and to improve their learning.

---

what a student might mean when offering an unusual interpretation of a short story.

Finally, the triple tensions of mindful teaching point to permanent dilemmas of teaching and learning that cannot ever be completely overcome, except for the briefest of moments. In many ways *they define the instructional situation*. It is your challenge to create a classroom environment that modulates the contradictions manifested in the triple tensions in a way that best serves your students, even as you remain mindful that in a given room there are many factors that you have not freely chosen but that you have been assigned with varying degrees of assent and coercion. Bringing the seven synergies to bear on the triple tensions so that they promote deep and sustainable learning is surely one of your most daunting tasks.

The Seven Synergies

1. *Open-mindedness* or "detachment from views" so that teachers practice seeing the validity of multiple perspectives on complicated issues related to curriculum choices or administrators' and policymakers' decisions;
2. A *caring and loving* disposition, so that teachers do not neglect the spiritual and emotional dimension of their vocation;
3. *Stopping*—either through formal meditation or informal reflection, so that teachers mitigate *reactivity* in favor of more considered *responsiveness*;
4. *Professional expertise*—respect for the entire ensemble of knowledge required of teachers today, spanning from the design and implementation of differentiated instruction, to communication with parents, to diverse modalities of studying and drawing inferences from pupil achievement data;
5. *Authentic alignment,* so that teachers make sure that their inner convictions and their outer practices are harmonized with one another and experienced as such by their students;
6. *Integration,* so that the whole range of pedagogical repertoires and choices are exploited and related to one another in the best interests of the students; and
7. *Collective responsibility,* so that teachers work on an ongoing basis with all social sectors to share appropriately in the education of the young.

The Triple Tensions

1. *Contemplation and action,* since one can always need more time to think just as one can always respond impulsively, but the real art of mindful teaching needs a carefully attuned integration of theory and practice;
2. *Ethics and power,* since a preoccupation with ethics can lead one to withdraw from the political sphere, and an excessive concern with power leads invariably to corruption and narcissism; and
3. The *individual and the collective,* since on some occasions a courageous individual is needed to overcome groupthink and to challenge the abuse of authority by school administrators, but in other instances individuals need to subordinate their own wishes to those of the majority out of respect for democratic processes and values.

In addition to the eightfold structure, the seven synergies, and the triple tensions, readers are invited to consider three levels of mindful teacher leadership. At the *microlevel,* you already are constantly revising and reflecting upon your educational interactions with children and young people. This is where your energies should be focused, and if at any point mindful teacher leadership distracts you from this core commitment, you must return to that axial relationship without which all else fails.

At the *mesolevel,* teacher groups that meet within and across schools invite opportunities for honing one's professional expertise and developing an integrative pedagogy. The Mindful Teacher seminars provided us with one free and independent setting for creating such a teacher network, and every district is characterized by a multitude of initiatives in this regard. Our central question for such initiatives, however, asks about the level of teacher ownership in either launching or steering a given network. No disrespect for administrators or external actors is intended, but our sense is that at this given historical moment teachers are especially needful of opportunities to bring forth their own ideas and to lead their own initiatives, with sympathetic yet also occasionally challenging outsiders as strategic allies.

Finally, while we agree with the numerous findings on teacher leadership that warn against reforms that take teachers too far away from their students, we also know that any situation where professors, administrators, and philanthropists regularly have opportunities to network at educational conferences, but teachers do not, cannot lead to the kinds of educational improvement we need today. As Andy Hargreaves has quipped, we can't have jet-setting school change *surfers* and classroom-bound teacher *serfs*! Teachers need forums like the International Conference of Teacher Researchers to share their professional growth as well as their challenges with one another. These forums or conferences provide venues for exploring and advocating *macrolevel* changes. Just as professors find validation outside of their universities by presenting their ideas and research to colleagues from other higher education institutions, so do teachers need those opportunities for professional renewal and growth. These need to entail not just listening and taking in information, but also submitting one's own ideas to the test in the court of professional opinion.

TEACHING AS A SPIRITUAL PRACTICE

In his lectures at the University of Berlin, Friedrich Schleiermacher (1826/2000) defended what he referred to as "the dignity of pedagogy" (p. 13) in transmitting the cultural heritage of humanity to a rising generation. For Schleiermacher, teaching was a spiritual act, requiring the most exquisite attention to the choice of instructional approaches, the selection of curricula, and attunement to the developing child's interests and needs. Always historically and culturally conditioned, it was the responsibility of educators to develop their own intellectual capabilities to their fullest, continually alert to the reality that their instruction would have impacts upon the young that extended far beyond the acquisition of skills or the completion of finite tasks.

In the decades following Schleiermacher's lectures, American reformers began adapting all kinds of Germanic innovations to our own radically different circumstances, with everything from kindergartens, graded schools, teacher training institutes, and research universities very much derived from Germanic antecedents. American thinkers such as the Transcendentalists (whose name derived from Immanuel Kant's transcendental philosophy), civil rights activist and educator W. E. B. DuBois (who studied at the University of Berlin), and progressive educator John Dewey all drew upon this intellectual heritage, extending and modulating it here on the other side of the Atlantic.

Yet while this embrace of a humanistic philosophy of education swept through so many niches and corners of American society, other tendencies were also underway. The "feminization" of education in the United States—meaning the rise of a predominantly female teaching force in schools—was conjoined with a predominantly male research presence in universities (Lagemann, 2002). Adapting experimental research designs from the natural sciences and applying them to schools, researchers began a century-long process of the objectification of teachers (Labaree, 2006). While research has contributed to the improvement of educational practice in many ways, the very real power differentials between professors and teachers have endured and persistently troubled the educational profession. As teachers have become more and more inundated by wave after wave of reform, their own opportunities to shape and define the profession have been thwarted. Teaching as a kind of spiritual practice, along lines articulated by Schleiermacher, has been almost entirely marginalized from contemporary American education.

Yet just when one might consider contemporary trends to be irreversible, countervailing tendencies have emerged. The contemporary financial crisis is prompting not just a rush to bail out the biggest banks, but also an exploration of the moral judgments that led policy makers and the public to ignore early warnings of impending danger (Soros, 2008). The intellectual skills of the most talented economists and statisticians were exposed as woefully inadequate when it came to the anticipation of our recession (Taleb, 2007). Increasingly, the wisest business leaders and change advocates (Fullan, 2008; Sisodia, Wolfe, & Sheth, 2007) understand that the full range of human intelligence and not just "reactive problem solving" (Senge et al., 2008, p. 50) will be needed to meet the challenges that lie ahead.

In education, this new appreciation for the complexity of change processes points us not just beyond what policy analysts have described as the "first way" of the 1960s welfare state and the "second way" of standardization and markets of the 1980s. It even points us beyond the policy arguments for a "third way" (Giddens, 1998, 2000) that aspired to unite the best of the first and second ways, but in education only came to do so by placing a historically unprecedented level of confidence in testing and accountability as levers of change. As has been argued elsewhere (Hargreaves & Shirley, 2009a) an unintended consequence of the third way as it became manifested in practice was to distract educators from their true purposes. Educators and the communities in which they were embedded experienced a "decline of the local" (Foster, 2004, p. 176) accompanied by the rise of government "deliverology" as an ideology (Barber, 2007, p. 70). Such policies conveyed little confidence that the self-initiated changes of teachers, parents, and community members could improve education.

In this context, mindful teaching and mindful teacher leadership must be understood not as outliers or distracters from government policies but rather as essential components of an emerging "fourth way" of change that acknowledges just how demanding and multifaceted teaching is today. In this new era teaching must go beyond addictive kinds of presentism that push us into short-term thinking, and instead recover the full grandeur, drama, and mystery of what it means to be one human soul educating another. It will mean finding in that instant of communication between teacher and student a spark of the divine, however obscure and misunderstood. It will mean delving as deeply into our common humanity and sharing that spiritual adventure with all of those students who are counting on us to help them to realize all of the latent treasures that lie untapped deep within.

References

Abrahamson, E. (2004). *Change without pain.* Cambridge, MA: Harvard Business School Press.

Achinstein, B. (2002). *Community, diversity, and conflict among schoolteachers: The ties that blind.* New York: Teachers College Press.

Anyon, J. (2005). *Radical possibilities: Public policy, urban education, and a new social movement.* New York: Routledge.

Austin, J. H. (1998). *Zen and the brain: Toward an understanding of meditation and consciousness.* Cambridge, MA: MIT Press.

Bailey, B. (2000). The impact of mandated change on teachers. In N. Bascia & A. Hargreaves (Eds.), *The sharp edge of educational change: Teaching, leading, and the realities of reform* (pp. 112–128). RoutledgeFalmer: New York.

Barber, M. (2007). *Instruction to deliver.* London: Methuen.

Begley, S. (2007). *Train your mind, change your brain.* New York: Ballantine.

Benard, B. (2006). Using strength-based practice to tap the resilience of families. In D. Saleebey (Ed.), *Strengths perspective in social work practice* (pp. 197–220). Boston: Allyn & Bacon.

Benedict, R. (1934). *Patterns of culture.* New York: Houghton Mifflin.

Blankstein, A., Houston, P., & Cole, R. (Eds.). (2008). *Sustaining professional learning communities.* Thousand Oaks, CA: Corwin.

Booher-Jennings, J. (2005). Below the bubble: "Educational triage" and the Texas accountability system. *American Educational Research Journal, 42*(2), 231–268.

Borko, H., Liston, D., & Whitcomb, J. A. (2007). Apples and fishes: The debate over dispositions in teacher education. *Journal of Teacher Education, 58*(5), 359–364.

Bridgeland, J. M., DiIulio, J. J., & Morison, K. B. (2006). *The silent epidemic: Perspectives of high school dropouts.* Washington, DC: Civic Enterprises.

Brisk, M. E., Dawson, M., Haertgering, M., MacDonald, E., & Zehr, L. (2002). Teaching bilingual students in mainstream classrooms. In: Z. Beykont (Ed.), *The power of culture* (pp. 89–120). Cambridge, MA: Harvard Education Publishing.

Bryk, A. S., Lee, V. E., Holland, P. B. (1993). *Catholic schools and the common good.* Cambridge, MA: Harvard University Press.

Bryk, A. S., & Schneider, B. L. (2004). *Trust in schools: A core resource for improvement.* New York: Russell Sage Foundation.

Campbell, E. (2005). Challenges in fostering ethical knowledge as professionalism within schools as teaching communities. *Journal of Educational Change, 6*(3), 207–226.

Celio, M. B., & Harvey, J. (2005). *Buried treasure: Developing an effective management guide from mountains of educational data.* Seattle: Center on Reinventing Public Education.

Chen, E., Heritage, M., & Lee, J. (2005). Identifying and monitoring students' learning needs with technology. *Journal of Education for Students Placed at Risk, 10*(3), 309–332.

Cochran-Smith, M., & Lytle, S. L. (1993) *Inside/Outside: Teacher research and knowledge.* New York: Teachers College Press.

Cochran-Smith, M., & Lytle, S. L. (2009) *Inquiry as stance: Practitioner research in the next generation.* New York: Teachers College Press.

Cohen, D. K. (1990). A revolution in one classroom: The case of Mrs. Oublier. *Educational Evaluation and Policy Analysis, 12*(3), 327–345.

Craig, C. (2006). Why is dissemination so difficult? The nature of teacher knowledge and the spread of curriculum reform. *American Educational Research Journal, 43*(2), 257–293.

Cripe, F. (1986). Rock music as therapy for children with attention deficit disorder: An exploratory study. *Journal of Music Therapy, 23*(1), 30–37.

Cusick, P. A. (2002). *A study of Michigan's principal shortage.* East Lansing: Education Policy Center, Michigan State University.

Darling-Hammond, L. (1990). Instructional policy into practice: "The power of the bottom over the top." *Educational Evaluation and Policy Analysis, 12*(3), 339–347.

Dewey, J. (1916). *Democracy and education.* New York: Free Press.

Dewey, J. (1938). *Experience and education.* New York: Collier.

Dynarski, M. (2008). Researchers and educators: Allies in learning. *Phi Delta Kappan, 66*(4), 48–53.

Evans, R. (2001). *The human side of school change: Reform, resistance, and the real-life problems of innovation.* San Francisco: Jossey-Bass.

Formisano, R. P. (1991). *Boston against busing: Race, class, and ethnicity in the 1960s and 1970s.* Chapel Hill: University of North Carolina Press.

Foster, W. P. (2004). The decline of the local: A challenge to educational leadership. *Educational Administration Quarterly, 40*(176), 176-191.

Freire, P. (2000). *Pedagogy of the oppressed.* New York: Continuum.

Fried, R. L. (1995). *The passionate teacher: A practical guide.* Boston: Beacon Press.

Friedman, A. (2004). Beyond mediocrity: Transformational leadership within a transactional framework. *International Journal of Leadership in Education, 7*(3), 203–224.

Frisina, W. G. (2002). *The unity of knowledge and action: Toward a nonrepresentational theory of knowledge.* Albany: State University of New York Press.

Fullan, M. (2001). *The new meaning of educational change* (3rd ed.). New York: Teachers College Press.

Fullan, M. (2008). *The six secrets of change: What the best leaders do to help their organizations survive and thrive.* San Francisco: Jossey-Bass.

Gardner, H., Csikszentmihalyi, M., & Damon, W. (2001) *Good work: When excellence and ethics meet.* New York: Basic Books.

Giddens, A. (1998). *The third way: The renewal of social democracy.* Cambridge: Polity.

Giddens, A. (2000). *The third way and its critics.* Cambridge: Polity.

Hamilton, L. S., Stecher, B. M., Marsh, J. A., McCombs, J. S., Robyn, A., Russell, J. L., Naftel, S., & Barney, H. (2007). *Standards-based accountability under No Child Left Behind: Experiences of teachers and administrators in three states.* Santa Monica, CA: RAND.

Hanh, T. N. (1988). *The heart of understanding.* Berkeley, CA: Parallax Press.

Hanh, T. N. (1992). *The diamond that cuts through illusion.* Berkeley, CA: Parallax Press.

Hanh, T. N. (1998). *Interbeing: Fourteen guidelines for engaged Buddhism.* Berkeley, CA: Parallax Press.

Hanh, T. N. (2001). *Essential writings.* Maryknoll, NY: Orbis.

Hanh, T. N. (2005). *Keeping the peace: Mindfulness and public service.* Berkeley, CA: Parallax Press.

Hargreaves, A. (1994). *Changing teachers, changing times: Teachers work and culture in the postmodern age.* New York: Teachers College Press.

Hargreaves, A. (2002). Teaching and betrayal. *Teachers and Teaching: Theory and Practice, 13*(4), 393–407.

Hargreaves, A. (2003). *Teaching in the knowledge society: Education in the age of insecurity.* New York: Teachers College Press.

Hargreaves, A. (2004). Inclusive and exclusive educational change: Emotional responses of teachers and implications for leadership. *School Leadership and Management, 24* (2), 287–309.

Hargreaves, A., & Fink, D. (2006). *Sustainable leadership.* San Francisco: Jossey-Bass.

Hargreaves, A., Halász, G., & Pont, B. (2008). The Finnish approach to system leadership. In: B. Pont, D. Nusche, & D. Hopkins (Eds.), *Improving school leadership, Vol. 2: Case studies on system leadership* (pp. 69–109). Paris: OECD.

Hargreaves, A., & Shirley, D. (2008). Beyond standardization: Powerful new principles for improvement. *Phi Delta Kappan, 90*(2), 135–143.

Hargreaves, A., & Shirley, D. (2009a) *The fourth way: The inspiring future of educational change.* Thousand Oaks, CA: Corwin.

Hargreaves, A., & Shirley, D. (2009b). The persistence of presentism. *Teachers College Record, 111*(11).

Hargreaves, A., Shirley, D., Evans, M., Stone-Johnson, C., & Riseman, D. (2007). *The long and short of school improvement: Final evaluation of the Raising Achievement Transforming Learning Programme of the Specialist Schools and Academies Trust.* London: Specialist Schools and Academies Trust.

Harris, A. (2008) *Distributed school leadership: Developing tomorrow's leaders.* London: Routledge.

Hewitt, P., Pijanowski, J., Carnine, L., & Denny, G. (2008). *The status of school leadership in Arkansas.* Fayetteville: University of Arkansas.

Hopkins, D. (2001). *School improvement for real.* New York: RoutledgeFalmer.

Huberman, M. (1993) *The lives of teachers.* New York: Teachers College Press.

Huberman, M. (1999). The mind is its own place: The influence of sustained interactivity with practitioners on educational researchers. *Harvard Educational Review, 69*(3), 289–319.

Ingersoll, R. M. (2003). *Who controls teachers' work? Power and accountability in America's schools.* Cambridge, MA: Harvard University Press.

Ingram, D., Seashore Louis, K., & Schroeder, R. G. (2004). Accountability policies and teacher decision making: Barriers to the use of data to improve practice. *Teachers College Record, 106*(6), 1258–1287.

King, P. M, & Kitchener, K. S. (1994). *Developing reflective judgment: Understanding and promoting intellectual growth and critical thinking in adolescents and adults.* San Francisco: Jossey-Bass.

Klingberg, L. (1990). *Lehrende und Lernende im Unterricht: Zur didaktischen Aspekten ihrer Positionen im Unterrichtsprozeß.* Berlin: Volk und Wissen.

Labaree, D. F. (2004). *The trouble with ed schools.* New Haven: Yale University Press.

Lagemann, E. C. (2000). *An elusive science: the troubling history of educational research.* Chicago: University of Chicago.

Lane, R. E. (2000). *The loss of happiness in market democracies.* New Haven, CT: Yale University Press.

Langer, E. J. (1989). *Mindfulness.* Reading, MA: Addison-Wesley

Langer, E. J. (1997). *The power of mindful learning.* Reading, MA: Addison-Wesley.

Lantieri, L. (2008). *Building emotional intelligence.* Boulder, CO: Sounds True.

Leithwood, K., Jantzi, D., & Steinbach, R. (1999). *Changing leadership for changing times.* Buckingham, UK: Open University Press.

Lieberman, A., & Miller, L. (2004) *Teacher leadership.* San Francisco: Jossey-Bass.

Lieberman, A., & Miller, L. (2008) (Eds.) *Teachers in professional communities: Improving teaching and learning.* New York: Teachers College Press.

Lieberman, A., & Wood, D. R. (2003) *Inside the National Writing Project: Connecting network learning and classroom teaching.* New York: Teachers College Press.

Lima, J.A. (2001). Forgetting about friendship: Using conflict in teacher communities as a catalyst for school change. *Journal of Educational Change, 2,* 97–122.

Liston, D. P. & Zeichner, K. M. (1990). Reflective teaching and action research in preservice teacher education. *Journal of Education for Teaching, 16*(3), 235–254.

Little, J. W., & Bartlett, L. (2002). Career and commitment in the context of comprehensive school reform. *Theory and Practice, 8*(3), 345–354.

Lortie, D. (1975) *Schoolteacher: A sociological study.* Chicago: University of Chicago Press.

Maathai, W. (2003). *The green belt movement: Sharing the approach and the experience.* Brooklyn: Lantern.

Marx, K. (1978). Economic and philosophical manuscripts. In: R. C. Tucker (Ed.), *The Marx-Engels reader* (pp. 66–125). New York: Norton. (Original work published 1844)

Maslow, A.H. (1969) *The psychology of science: A reconnaissance.* Chicago: Gateway.

McDonald, J. P., Mohr, N., Dichter, A., & McDonald, E. (2007). *The power of protocols: An educator's guide to better practice.* New York: Teachers College Press.

McLaughlin, M. W. (2006). Implementation research in education: Lessons learned, lingering questions and new opportunities. In: M. I. Honig (Ed.), *New directions in education policy implementation: Confronting complexity.* Albany: State University of New York Press.

McLaughlin, M. W., & Talbert, J. (2001). *Professional communities and the work of high school teaching.* Chicago: University of Chicago Press.

McQuillan, P.J. (1998) *Educational opportunity in an urban American high school: A cultural analysis.* Albany: State University of New York Press.

Mill, J.S. (1931). Inaugural address at St. Andrews. In: F.A. Cavenaugh (Ed.), *James and John Stuart Mill on education* (p. 32). Cambridge, MA: Harvard University Press.

Murphy, J., Goldring, E., & Porter, A. (2006). *Leadership for learning: A research-based model and taxonomy of behaviors.* Wallace Foundation State Action for Educational Leadership Conference, St. Louis, MO.

Murrell, P. C., Jr. (2001). *The community teacher: A new framework for effective urban teaching.* New York: Teachers College Press.

Newmann, F., & Wehlage, G. (1995). *Successful school restructuring.* Madison, WI: Center on Organization and Restructuring of Schools.

Nieto, S. (2003). *What keeps teachers going?* New York: Teachers College Press.

Noddings, N. (1992). *The challenge to care in schools.* New York: Teachers College Press.

Noddings, N. (2001). Care and coercion in school reform. *Journal of Educational Change, 2,* 35–43.

Noguera, P. A. (2008). *The trouble with black boys . . . and other reflections on race, equity, and the future of public education.* San Francisco: Jossey-Bass.

Oakes, J., Rogers, J., & Lipton, M. (2006). *Learning power: Organizing for education and justice.* New York: Teachers College Press.

Ogilby, H. (2007). Teacher leadership: Noble aspiration or myth? In R. H. Ackerman & S. V. Mackenzie (Eds.), *Uncovering teacher leadership* (pp. 161–166). Thousand Oaks, CA: Corwin Press.

Pallotta, F. (2004). *Freedom is an endless meeting: Democracy in American social movements.* Chicago: University of Chicago Press.

Palmer, P. J. (1998). *The courage to teach: Exploring the inner landscape of a teacher's life.* San Francisco: Jossey-Bass.

Payne, C. M. (2008). *So much reform, so little change.* Cambridge, MA: Harvard Education Press.

Payton, J., Weissberg, R. P., Durlak, J. A., Dymnicki, A. B., Taylor, R. D., Schellinger, K. B., & Pachan, M. (2008). *The positive impact of social and emotional learning for kindergarten to eighth-grade students: Findings from three scientific reviews.* Chicago: Collaborative for Academic, Social, and Emotional Learning.

Pedulla, J., Abrams, L. M., Madaus, G. F., Russell, M. K., Ramos, M. A., & Miao, J. (2003). *Perceived effects of state-mandated testing programs on teaching and learning: Findings from a national survey of teachers.* Chestnut Hill, MA: National Board on Educational Testing and Public Policy.

Perlstein, D. H. (2004). *Justice, justice: School politics and the eclipse of liberalism.* New York: Peter Lang.

Peterman, F. P. (Ed.). (2008). *Partnering to prepare urban teachers: A call to activism.* New York: Peter Lang:

Pressman, J. L., & Wildavsky, A. (1973). *Implementation: How great expectations in Washington are dashed in Oakland.* Berkeley: University of California Press.

Ravitch, D. (2000). *Left back: A century of failed school reform.* New York: Simon & Schuster.

Reville, S. P. (2007). (Ed.). *A decade of urban school reform: Persistence and progress in the Boston public schools.* Cambridge, MA: Harvard Education Press.

Rosenholtz, S. (1989). *Teachers' workplace.* New York: Longman.

Rusch, E. A. (2005). Institutional barriers to organizational learning in school systems: The power of silence. *Educational Administration Quarterly, 41*(1), 83–120.

Scheurich, J. J. (1998). Highly successful and loving, public elementary schools populated mainly by low SES children of color: Core beliefs and cultural characteristics. *Urban Education, 33*(4), 451–491.

Schleiermacher, F. (2000). *Texte zur Pädagogik* (Vol. 2). Frankfurt: Suhrkamp. (Original work published 1826)

Schön, D.A. (1987) *Educating the reflective practitioner: Toward a new design for teaching and learning in the professions.* San Francisco: Jossey-Bass.

Seligman, M. E. P. (2002). *Authentic happiness.* New York: Free Press.

Selman, M. (1988). Schoen's gate is square: But is it art? In P. P. Grimmett & G. I. Erickson (Eds.), *Reflection in teacher education* (pp. 177–192). New York : Teachers College Press.

Senge, P., Smith, B., Kruschwitz, N., Laur, J., & Schley, S. (2008). *The necessary revolution: How individuals and organizations are working together to create a sustainable world.* New York: Doubleday.

Shirley, D. (1997). *Community organizing for urban school reform.* Austin: University of Texas Press.

Shirley, D. (2002). *Valley Interfaith and school reform: Organizing for power in South Texas.* Austin: University of Texas Press.

Shirley, D. (2006a). The Massachusetts Coalition for Teacher Quality and Student Achievement: An introduction. *Excellence and Equity in Education, 39*(1), 4–14

Shirley, D. (2006b). Street-level democrats: Realizing the potential of school, university, and community coalitions. *The Education Forum, 70*(2), 116–122.

Shirley, D. (2008a). American perspectives on German educational theory and research: A closer look at both the American educational context and the German Didaktik tradition. In: K. H. Arnold, S. Blömeke, R. Messner, & J. Schlömerkemper (Eds.), *Allgemeine Didaktik und Lehr-Lernforschung: Kontrontroversen und Entwicklungsperspektiven einer Wissenschaft von Unterricht.* Paderborn: Klinkhardt.

Shirley, D. (2008b). The coming of post-standardization in education: What role for the German Didaktik tradition? *Zeitschrift für Erziehungswissenschaft, 10*(9), 35–46.

Shirley, D., & Hargreaves, A. (2006). Data-driven to distraction. *Education Week, 26*(4), 32–33.

Shirley, D., Hersi, A., MacDonald, E., Sanchez, M. T., Scandone, C., Skidmore, C., & Tutwiler, P. (2006). Bringing the community back in: Change, accommodation, and contestation in a school and university partnership. *Excellence and Equity in Education, 39*(1), 27–36.

Siegel, D. J. (2007). *The mindful brain: Reflection and attunement in the cultivation of well-being.* New York: Norton.

Sisodia, R. S., Wolfe, D. B., & Sheth, J. N. (2007). *Firms of endearment: How world-class companies profit from passion and purpose.* Upper Saddle River, NJ: Wharton School Publishing.

Snow, C., Burns, M. S., & Griffin, P. (1998). *Preventing reading difficulties in young children.* Washington, DC: National Academy Press.

Soros, G. (2008). *The new paradigm for financial markets.* New York: PublicAffairs.

Spellings Commission. (2006). *A test of leadership: Charting the future of U.S. higher education.* Washington, DC: U.S. Department of Education.

Spillane, J. P. (2006) *Distributed leadership.* San Francisco: Jossey-Bass.

Spillane, J. P., & Diamond, J. B. (2007). Taking a distributed perspective. In J. P. Spillane & J. B. Diamond (Eds.), *Distributed leadership in practice* (pp. 1–15). New York: Teachers College Press.

Stoll, L., Bolgam, R., McMahon, A., Wallace, M., & Thomas, S. (2006). Professional learning communities: A review of the literature. *Journal of Educational Change, 7*(4), 221–258.

Stoll, L., & Seashore Louis, K. (Eds.). (2007). *Professional learning communities: Divergence, depth and dilemmas.* Berkshire, UK: Open University Press.

Symonds, K. W. (2003). *After the test: How schools are using data to close the achievement gap.* San Francisco: Bay Area School Reform Collaborative.

Taleb, N. N. (2007). *The black swan: The impact of the highly improbable.* New York: Random House.

Tremmel, R. (1993). Zen and the art of reflective practice in teacher education. *Harvard Educational Review, 63*(4), 434–458.

Wallace, B. A. (Ed.). (2003). *Buddhism and science: Breaking new ground.* New York: Columbia University Press.

Welner, K. G. (2001). *Legal rights, local wrongs: When community control collides with educational equity.* Albany: State University of New York Press.

Westbury, I., Hopmann, S., & Riquarts, K. (2000). *Teaching as a reflective practice: The German Didaktik tradition.* Mahwah, NJ: Erlbaum.

Index

About the Authors

Elizabeth MacDonald is an elementary school teacher and teacher leader in the Boston Public Schools. **Dennis Shirley** is a professor of education at the Lynch School of Education at Boston College. Liz and Dennis have founded a seminar for urban teachers called "The Mindful Teacher," which provides educators with a collegial setting for combining teacher inquiry, formal meditation practices, and collaborative study of and contributions to research. For more information, please visit their Web site at www.mindfulteacher.com.